Mental

Toughness:

30 Days to Become Mentally Tough, Create Unbeatable Mind, Developed Self-Discipline, Self Confidence, Assertiveness, Executive Toughness, Willpower, Self-Esteem, Love and Compassion

Table of Contents

Introduction

Right now, "Mental Toughness" has become a buzzword shared on corporate retreats and accompanied by bad stock photos. I am sure right now you are picturing a mildly attractive blonde woman pointing at a board with graphs on it while her co-workers nod agreeably, or perhaps you've decided to go more metal and envisioned eroded graphics and a battlefield touting phrases like, "Leaders lead," and maybe there is even a wolf somewhere in the background. Hopefully, you are not thinking of a guy in a 90s business suit with his arms crossed as he looks, "ready to teach you how to be tough," with six easy steps.

The fact of the matter is there is a large market out there for playing to people's fantasies. We spin books like "How to Win Money and Lead with Confidence" and "Perception: The Secret to the Secret" to appeal to the vast amount of people who merely want to know how to be better.

And therein lies our quest. You want to be better at, something. Perhaps you are not even sure what it is, but you know that mentally you feel weak and perhaps this whole warrior mindset thing has some truth to it. Could you be Achilles?

Sadly, no, you are not Achilles, unless your parents named you Achilles which in that case, good luck; however, the other 99% of us who are not the most celebrated athletes/warriors on the planet have to find a way to be better, to accomplish our goals.

So, what do we do?

We learn.

Human beings are where we are today, both for the good and the bad, because we adapt. We see something is not working as well as it could, and we fix it. We look for duct tape, and we solve problems, sometimes we solve problems with duct tape, but then someone ultimately comes along and fixes what we were so desperately trying to hold together.

If your life is one series after another of duct tape solutions, then it is time to go back and sharpen the saw. The best thing we can do for ourselves is to teach ourselves how to learn and set up a new series of principles.

Thus, you are here. If you were hoping for slogans to lay on top of a cat hanging on to a rope, then you may have bought the wrong book. If, on the other hand, you want practical knowledge, keen examples, and actionable lessons then let's get started.

When we think of the keywords to describe mental toughness what comes to mind? Grit. Tenacity. Character.

In a broad stroke, mental toughness is the focus and willpower to complete your journey despite difficult obstacles. In other words, never give up.

In more minute detail, mental toughness is the willingness to make the tough choices, the strength to act, the ability to focus, the tenacity to deliver, and the power to carry the weight.

Perhaps you picture the cool and collected stoic overlooking a battlefield or a resilient entrepreneur leading a boardroom. Perhaps images of elite athletes trudging through hell and high water or Navy SEAL's pushing through BUDS appear in your psyche.

Whatever images come to mind, mental toughness represents the pinnacle of what we need to succeed. Yet, for all its praise, it is undoubtedly one of those skills that cannot be boiled down to 1's and 0's. The very trait of mental toughness is as unique as the people who possess it.

When we talk of success, rarely do we speak of the most talented. Often, we wish to surmise those people who reach the top are simply the most gifted, yet, time and time again this is not the case. Tom Brady is certainly not the most physically talented quarterback, neither was Michael Jordan, the most versatile basketball player at a young age. So, what gave them an edge? Mental toughness.

Take a note, talent is overrated. Those who become successful are those who learn to push beyond what they are capable of from the start.

First, what are some of the characteristics of the mentally strong? Courage and resolve, strength of character, Emotional stability, coolness under pressure, perspective and detachment, ability to perform on a dime, acceptance of change, versatility, preparation, discipline, focus, self-esteem, endurance, patience, tenacity, and purpose.

Mentally tough people learn to delay gratification until the goal is accomplished, and even then, grind daily, celebrate rarely. The mental strong learn to control fear and use it. They turn fear into a superpower, using it to guide their decisions and push their boundaries. They don't just prioritize, but they build their priorities around their purpose. In other words, people with grit develop their character to the level of greatness. How do you beat mistakes, you prepare?

As Bill Belichick says, "Talent sets the floor, character sets the ceiling." Mental strength carries you through the hard times when the whole world turns against you. It provides us a model to work through once the pressure is on.

Life is lived under pressure. The greatest moments do not wait for our leisure. We must learn to control the things in our power and accept the things we cannot change. Learn the lessons that will help you in the future and move on. Failure is a part of success. Grit is the fire in your belly that keeps burning even when everything goes wrong. It's the voice that talks you through those times and tells you to keep trying until you get it right. Never give up. Stay true to your course. Keep your standards high.

The question is: How do we get it?

1. What is mental toughness to you?

How do you define mental toughness? Is it the ability to rise to the challenge? Is it control? Is it commitment? Is confidence?

2. What are your goals and motivations?

The first step towards developing mental toughness is discovering what you are after. No one is going to give you what you want. You have to go after it yourself. You must be a self-starter. Define what you want and what your aim is.

3. What are you willing to sacrifice?

No one gets it all. To accomplish something, we must also give up something. We have known this since grade school. We must choose our priorities and in doing so decide what we must give up. Ancient civilizations would sacrifice lambs to the gods in order to protect the harvest, so to must we make a metaphorical sacrifice to our goal.

The goal of this book is to give you insights into what mental toughness is and how you can develop it by giving you sage counsel from some of history's toughest individuals. We will be equipping you with the ideas, practices, and stratagems to develop your mental toughness and execute in whatever world you live in: sports, business, art. Yet, no matter the wisdom offered in this book, nothing can be accomplished if you are lacking the two core principles for mental toughness: grit and consistency.

Mentally strong people put in the work every day. The learn to preserve because of the show-up day in and day out. In order to accomplish anything, we must maintain. Wisdom is not gained without sacrifice. Therefore, in order to learn mental toughness, we must develop a new habit and be consistent with our effort.

Winston Churchill once said, "Success is not final, failure is not fatal: it is the courage to continue that counts."

How to Read This Book:

Congratulations, you are one step closer to developing your mental toughness. I say one step because that is how this journey is walked, one step at a time, one chapter at a time (unless, of course, you only read the "Key Takeaways" chapter and then walk away).

Either way, this book is both a readable document and a workbook. The chapters that follow will focus on mentally tough individuals and the lessons they offer us. I have chosen people such as David Goggins and Bill Belichick (sorry for those who hate him, but the man has more rings than Thanos) as well as characters such as Yoda and Sherlock Holmes.

The point is to offer you varying degrees of mental toughness as well as how it applies to different areas. Mental toughness has led warriors to victory over stronger opponents, and it has pushed individuals through Ironman races and weight loss. Mental strength, grit, and perseverance are better-determining factors for success than talent, access, and education.

So, how do you read this book?

First, you can read the following chapter and call it a day. It's a summary that gives you the quintessential lessons. If you are looking for something to bore your date with tonight or simply ran out of podcasts to talk about to your friends at work, then that's the one and only chapter you need.

Second, you can actually read the damn book. Simple, but effective. Since man discovered writing, there has been no better way to pass on knowledge than one man, or a group of men, putting one letter or figure after the other onto paper and then another person sitting silently by themselves consuming that information. If you are wondering, the answer is yes, I just described what reading is to you.

The book has 15 core chapters, each with an Actionable Step at the end. After each chapter is an accompanying short lesson for the following day.

The goal is to read a chapter every two days and do the Actionable Step throughout those two days. Why two days? Why not sit down and devour this book in one sitting? Well, you can if you want, but it's best to give things time.

We live in a world that wants results now. We want changes in an instant. We want miracle cures and fad diets over health and exercise. Mental toughness is like developing calluses on your brain, and the only way to do that is through hard work and habit.

You already possess so much potential by merely living the life you have lived or survived, and it is now time to build on that potential. To do that, give yourself the time necessary to make the change.

We see the flower when it buds just like we see the celebrity when they become an overnight success. Both took weeks, months, or years to flower and marketing sold it as an overnight success.

Furthermore, in this book are lessons you are likely to have heard a thousand times. I pull on clichés such as "Defense Wins Championships" and "Hard work builds success." Why do such ardent clichés make their way into a book written for internet in 2019, because timeless wisdom makes it ways down through the centuries for a reason? I guarantee you a knight was sitting on top a horse five hundred years ago screaming at his students about how "Blocking wins battles."

Sometimes, things stick. If they do, use them. Ponder on them, rewrite them, elaborate on them, analyze them, and ultimately make them your own, but by all means, use them.

After each initial chapter, there is a new thought for the next day. While I want you to focus on the lessons from the previous chapter, a follow-up thought is offered for you to marinate on.

Lastly, this book is about you. For the most part, I try to stay out of it. I am not your guru. I am not going to fix you. I am going to give you the tools to become stronger, but I am not going to provide you with a magic book of tricks that will turn you into Bruce Lee overnight.

I can't change who you are, but you can.

Key Takeaways:

Don't have time actually to read a book, be it on your Kindle, iPhone, or tablet? Well, then this is the one, and only, chapter for you.

Listed below are the key takeaways, sans Actionable steps, from each section with a short lesson listed under each. This way, when you arrive at work today, you can still carry something intelligent into the meeting.

Chapter 1: Get Your Mind Right, A Lesson from Bruce Lee

Make a choice to start today. The mind dictates to the body. To accomplish anything, we must get in the right headspace. Mental toughness is as much about mindset as it is about toughness. Sometimes, the strength to sit with a problem is the strength to solve it. Stop thinking everything should be solvable by Google and start gearing yourself up for the big decisions.

Chapter 2: The Journey Before You. A Lesson from Joseph Campbell

Life is a journey. We all know this. But we don't quite understand it as well as the man who studied myth his whole life and found out that every culture tells a similar tale he dubbed the "monomyth." This discovery led to the creation of such stories as Star Wars and The Matrix. The lesson to be learned is that if we approach our lives as the journey that it is, rather than some mundane curse, and we follow our bliss or real purpose, then the trials of life become more bearable. We discover what dragon we must face and what prize we must seek.

Chapter 3: Set Your Goal, A Lesson from Zig Ziglar

The master orator Zig Ziglar was one of the earliest self-help gurus who transcended the genre, and for a good reason. He's funny, witty, and right. His biggest lesson? Set your goal (your bliss) and remind yourself daily of what you want. Develop mantras and affirmations to drive your desires into your subconscious. Motivation is like bathing, we must do it every day. Affirmations are brain training. If you want to build a stricter mind, it starts with training the brain to think differently.

Chapter 4: Write It Down, A Lesson from Tim Ferris and the Five-Minute Journal

One of the best ways to retrain your brain is to write. There has yet to be created a more powerful tool of changing your perspective than putting pen to paper. Tim Ferris is famous for a lot of things: he has a brilliant podcast, several best sellers including "The 4-Hour Workweek," and has developed a brand around being a Lifehacker and dilatant. His greatest discovery? There are a lot, but my personal favorite tool is Julia Cameron's Five-Minute Morning Pages. Since this is the short version, sit down every morning for five minutes and write your thoughts down. Do not judge what you write, just write it and forget it.

Chapter 5: You are Going to Fail, A Lesson from David Goggins

Failure is a part of success. No one who has accomplished anything has ever done it on a perfect wave. David Goggins is one of the most badass people on the planet. How do I know? Listen to an interview with him or read his book and will tell you so; however, the man backs it up. He's demolished Ironman's as well as his biceps while breaking the record for pull-ups. The most important lesson he has to offer us? Whether its long-running distances, pushing your body through extreme heat, or building a business, on the journey towards your goal you are going to get it wrong at some point and fail. This is a gift. We learn more from losing than winning, and the only way to get to the top of the mountain is to learn and do it again, but better.

Chapter 6: Meditation, from Tennis to Tatooine

If writing is the best tool for developing mental strength, then meditation is the best cardio workout. This simple habit has been practiced by people for centuries, and yet it is coming back into vogue recently. In the world we live in today, with constant access to entertainment and data, our brains are becoming overheated, and we need a way to hit reset. Athletes have learned that the focus required of the game and the flow state is similar to the mindset of monks deep in meditation. Use this tool to focus your mind and gain back some of your free space.

Chapter 7: Ask Questions, A Lesson from Toyota

Why? Why? Why? Why? Why? Five times. The gift from Toyota is a shovel to dig into your psyche. It forces you to go deeper into your thought process, your failures, your successes and learn why you did what you did and how do you make it better.

Chapter 8: Carry that Weight, A Lesson from Jordan Peterson

In life, we make choices. Every choice we make carries a weight. No matter what we do, no matter who we are, we all must bear the burden of our decisions. To live a better life, do not do anything that would make you feel shame. If you do, or if you have, accept your burden, but understand that if you wish to put your life in order, it begins with you and your choices. Also, read great literature if you want to understand hot perils of life.

Chapter 9: Master the Grunt Work, A Lesson from Bill Belichick

No days off. Belichick chanted this from the podium after he won his fifth championship. The coach who everyone hates got to the top of the mountain by doing the work no one else wanted to do. If you are an actor, you memorize lines not go to parties. If you are a writer, you sit alone and do the work. Success is built on the back of hard work. Plain and simple, like Belichick.

Chapter 10: Perseverance, A Lesson from Winston Churchill

The British Bulldog led his country through the most trying time in history. While we may not face the blitzkrieg in our life, we will undoubtedly feel like life is throwing everything it's got at us. If you are going through hell, keep going. This too shall pass.

Chapter 11: Discipline Equals Freedom, A Lesson from Jocko Willink

Harping back to Dr. Peterson, the more discipline we develop life, from making our bed to daily exercise, the more freedom we will begin to discover. Pulling lessons from the military, choices often shackle us, we are imprisoned by options. The more disciplined we are today, the more time we will have tomorrow. A man with no time is a man with no priorities.

Chapter 12: Embrace the Obstacle, A Lesson from Stoicism

While this could be seen as a repeat from Campbell, the stoics, technically, came first. Life sucks if you look at it that way. If you change your mindset and realize that the obstacle in your path is your path, then suddenly your burden becomes your purpose. The barrier is the way as Ryan Holiday quotes.

Chapter 13: Success, a Lesson from Coach K

Integrity. No scandals. No suspensions. No time spent on the cover of The National Enquirer. Coach K has done it right over his long successful career. He leads with integrity, be it the Duke Blue Devils of the Olympic team. He learns to adapt and change with the times, starting with strong Senior leadership and then adopting the One and Done players later in his career, but always taking the best players and teaching them to play the game the right way. When you have integrity, when you know what you stand for, success is predetermined, because you know who you are.

Chapter 14: Carry Two Swords, A Lesson from Musashi

Always be prepared. Often, Plan A doesn't work. Therefore, you must carry a second sword. While there is more to Musashi than that, you wanted the short version.

Chapter 15: The Training, A Lesson from Sherlock Holmes

Your brain operates on two levels when faced with new information: fast and slow. Train your mind to connect the two, so that your quick reactions are based on your slow analysis, like Holmes. You do this by, at first, creating distance from the problem at hand and slowly thinking through the possibilities. Over time, what was slow will become fast. It's the way the human body works. Think of a fighter in a ring who does not think but moves from muscle memory.

Conclusion: You are Enough

Go to, and kick ass. Like every hero on every journey, the ultimate quest is the one that takes place within. We were enough to conquer the mountain or the dragon, or both, and claim the prize, but we needed the journey to teach us that. So too are you enough. You always were. Still, you need to practice and develop, because one day you will need to pass on what you know.

Chapter 1:

"If you spend too much time thinking about a thing, you'll never get it done. Make at least one definite move daily toward your goal."
Bruce Lee

This is not about me inspiring you. When it comes down to it, you are either ready to change, or you or not. You are ready to get stronger, or you are not. You are prepared to take the plunge, or you are not.

I wish I could tell you there is a magical secret at the end of the book, or that absolutely, 100% money back guarantee, that at the end of 30 Days you will be a changed man or woman.

I wish I could bark at you with carnival sincerity that if you follow this step by step guide, you will come out the other side stronger, sexier, and with thicker, fuller hair.

I wish I could tell you that after reading this book the world will be a better place and that it's not going to Hell in a handbasket.

But, I can't. The truth is it's entirely up to you.

Certainly, in this book, you will find hacks, quotes, and how to's. You will find daily inspiration and steps you can take to start kicking ass and taking names. I guarantee it.

Still, what I cannot promise is that book jacket tagline, late-night infomercial empty pitch, because we both know who it is up to.

And yet, you have already taken the first step. You have made a choice to invest in yourself and grow.

Stanford psychologist Carol Dweck, the author of The New Psychology of Success, pushes the idea of the "growth mindset," or the belief that our intellect, creativity, and character all can adapt and change for the better. We are not set in our ways, we are ever evolving, learning machines.

As you have grown older, how have you changed? If you were to exclude the physical, what are the new mental models you have adapted that have produced positive results? Are you the same person you were in high school?

There are two approaches, according to Dweck, fixed and growth. When presented with a problem, a person falls into one of two interpretations. They either struggle or fail and say, "I am so stupid, I shouldn't even bother trying," or, "I haven't mastered this yet, but I will, given time and knowledge."

These two thoughts result in dramatically different outcomes. Imagine saying to yourself day in and day out, "I am dumb," or, "I am just like X," or even, "I suck. I am a failure."

Do you give up easily? Do you avoid failure? Do you despise criticism? Is the success of others a threat to your success?

This is a fixed mindset.

What if your best friend said these things to you every single day? How much of a friend would they be? And yet, we have no problem lambasting ourselves with this hate speech any time we come up short in our lives.

It ends today.

We have built the habit of poor self-talk, and it's not going to go away in an hour. But, today is the day that we are going to pay attention to it and shift our thoughts towards a growth mindset.

Rather than kicking ourselves when we encounter an obstacle, we are going to change the flow of energy to thoughts such as, "I need to work smarter," or, "I will get it next time," or even, "This is going to be fun."

Be open to new ideas, to change. Understand that you can always learn and grow. Reflect upon the challenge, learn from the lesson, and allow yourself to build from experience.

The truth is, life has gotten comfortable. We no longer have to struggle the way our forefathers did. Want a burger? Well, we used to have to hunt down and stalk the calf before we could eat. Today, we hop on our phone and order from

GrubHub, complaining if it wasn't delivered in under 30 minutes.

This sort of lethargy has seeped into our minds. We expect immediate results. We expect knowledge without investment. We expect success without tribulation.

Arnold Schwarzenegger did not start out as The Terminator. Dwayne ", The Rock" Johnson, did not make the NFL, which was his initial dream. Comedians such as Joe Rogan, Kevin Hart, and Dave Chapelle have talked again and again about the long road to being funny.

Thank about that for a second. Comedy is hard. Something we do every single day, laugh and smile when putting under the microscope and expected to work every time, is hard. The best in the world at standing on a stage and making people laugh tell us time in and time out, that writing jokes is a science.

Serious people win in comedy. While we want to believe it is the class clown that follows his heart to Comedy Store, more often than not it is the person who takes the art of writing jokes and the craft of delivering them night after night seriously that succeed in comedy.

Jerry Seinfeld writes a joke every day. He has a large calendar on his wall. Each day he writes a joke he puts an 'X' through the day. This way, he can see when he breaks the chain and when he is on a roll. Dave Chappelle puts random punchlines into a bowl and then draws one out every day.

Before the days over, he has to come up with a joke to the punchline.

If writing jokes are science and being swole didn't come at the end of a needle, then where does that leave us?

As Hunter S. Thompson said, "Buy the ticket, take the ride."

Our journey begins.

Actionable Steps:

-The journey of a thousand miles begins with the first step, but actually, it begins with the choice to take the step. Make the choice to get in the right frame of mind to become mentally tougher

Day 2: Focus

"Whenever you want to achieve something, keep your eyes open, concentrate and make sure you know exactly what it is you want. No one can hit their target with their eyes closed." - Paulo Coelho

Learning how to focus in a world that craves your attention is crucial. Unplugging can be vital to discovering your abilities. It's not only knowing what we want but learning how to get it. Sometimes, it can be as simple as getting the voices out of your head. Today, take time to be with yourself. No podcasts. No news. No audiobooks. No social media. Just you. Pay attention to your thoughts. Observe them. If you feel the need, write them down, but enjoy the silence of the day.

Chapter 2:

"The big question is whether you are going to be able to say a hearty yes to your adventure." -Joseph Campbell

You are the hero of your own story.

Joseph Campbell was an American mythologist, writer, and lecturer, best known for his work in comparative mythology and comparative religion and the book "The Hero with a Thousand Faces," that would later influence George Lucas's Star Wars. He is also the philosopher who coined the phrase, "Follow your bliss."

His writings are dense, but his message is simple. In all the stories human beings have been telling is a congruent monomyth. All our heroes are on the same journey from Gilgamesh and Odysseus to Luke and Dorothy.

Why is this included in this book? Myths provide guidance for difficult times. They can offer advice, lessons, and examples as we struggle to survive our own ordeals. In essence, the myths we read in books or see in movies become our mentors for how to deal with turbulent times.

Furthermore, you are on a journey. You have set out to become mentally stronger, and there is no better metaphor to understand when facing challenges than the monomyth. We all have our favorite heroes: Batman, Bond, Sherlock, Wolverine, Wonder Woman. If we can learn from their journey and experience our own, then we are on the way to experiencing life.

"Only a fool learns from his own mistakes. The wise man learns from the mistakes of others." -Otto von Bismarck

The call to adventure.

In the beginning, we all find ourselves in the ordinary world: the village, the small town, the 9 to 5. The Hero is just like you and me, he has dreams and aspirations of something greater but is trapped by the chains of his surroundings. If only something would come along to stir up this provincial life, if only.

"Your life is the fruit of your own doing. You have no one to blame but yourself." -Joseph Campbell

This is Luke longing to join the Rebellion but finding himself stuck on Tatooine; however, when he sees two new droids the call to adventure has begun. One is carrying a message for Obi-Wan that will change the course of Luke's life; however, one key component of Campbell's monomyth is the "refusal of the call." Meaning, our hero, time and time again, try to hold on to the Ordinary World. They work and play it safe for as long as they can. Even Luke Skywalker who we all now know is destined to become the next Jedi, finds an excuse to stay on Tatooine, however, once he returns home, he finds that fate has nudged him towards adventure as his Aunt and Uncle have been slain by the Empire.

Will you answer the call?

Supernatural aid. Meeting the mentor.

The hero now needs guidance. The person they are today is not the hero who is ready to face the Shadow. At this point, our hero needs a mentor, someone who holds an object, information, advice, or understands a lost art. Think Gandalf, Morpheus, or even a simple college professor. Whoever the mentor is and whatever knowledge they possess, their mission is to pass it on to the hero so they may continue their quest.

Obi-Wan possesses the lightsaber, the weapon of an ancient sect of warriors the Jedi, of Luke's father. He is also the person Princess Leia seeks to save the Rebellion.

"Follow your bliss and the universe will open doors for you where there were only walls." - Joseph Campbell

The point is, none of us are ready to achieve our goals yet. Self-help and positive thinking would have you believe that all you need is the right mindset and the world is your oyster. And to be fair, they are not wrong.

Yes, you do need the right mindset to accomplish your goals, however, simply changing your frame of mind is not suddenly going to make you a starting linebacker or teach you how to play chess or fence.

We need mentors; however, a mentor can be anything from a teacher to an Book. Today, we have more access to information than ever before. There are YouTube channels dedicated to teaching people, websites with courses that used to belong only to elite universities, and podcasts touting hours and hours of interviews, investigations, and audio essays.

So, even if you can't find your Obi-Wan, you can find people willing to share their secrets. Once you make the choice to become tougher, open your mind to the possibilities of learning. When the student is ready, the teacher will appear.

Crossing the threshold. Trials and tribulations.

Once the choice has been made and the call answered, the Hero is ready to begin his quest. Sometimes it is willingly, sometimes the hero is pushed. As Shakespeare wrote, "Be not afraid of greatness: some are born great, some achieve greatness, and some have greatness thrust upon them."

Either way, the hero now enters an unfamiliar world. It can be Odysseus crossing into the Underworld, Luke making the jump to outer space with Han, or even Rick and Morty going on some crazy adventure (note that creator of Rick and Morty Dan Harmon loves the monomyth and has created his own version that every episode is based on).

"We must be willing to get rid of the life we've planned, so as to have the life that is waiting for us." - Joseph Campbell

Crossing the threshold signifies the Hero's commitment to his journey and whatever it may have in store for him; however, once the jump is made trials and tribulations wait, for the hero must be tested before they face the ultimate challenge. Furthermore, what once worked will not continue to work for the hero, and they must learn new skills from the Mentor to move forward in their journey.

Onboard the Millennium Falcon with Luke and Chewy, Luke must immediately fight Tai fighters from the Empire. We learn that Luke is more than capable of defending himself as a pilot and sharpshooter and that he is fully committed to saving the princess.

Once safe, we next see Obi-Wan teaching Luke the ways of the Force. Obi-Wan knows the grit and determination of Luke will not be enough for the trials ahead, and that if either of them is to succeed Luke must learn a greater skill.

"A hero is someone who has given his or her life to something bigger than oneself." - Joseph Campbell

The Abyss, The Ordeal, and The Transformation.

The hero is fully out of his comfort zone and will be confronted with challenges that are more difficult. Obstacles present themselves, and only those worthy of the challenge will overcome.

Furthermore, the Hero must find allies. He must learn who to trust and who not to. In Star Wars, Luke develops a bond with Han and Chewy as they save the Princess (who becomes an even greater ally), and he loses Obi-Wan to Darth Vader.

For the hero, greater trials lie ahead, and it is here that the greatest meat of the story resides. Structurally speaking, we are in Acts 3 or 4 in the story, the middle of the book. Often, the Hero becomes lost, much like the reader, in their journey. What once seemed clear and easy is not despairing and insurmountable.

"The cave you fear to enter holds the treasure you seek." -Joseph Campbell

It is often what we fear most that hold the greatest reward. Conquering our fears is more than just a psychological exercise used by doctors. In primitive cultures, something Campbell studied extensively, every child must face a great dragon before they are allowed to enter into adulthood.

What does this have to do with anything? Dragons are the creation of all of man's primal fears: tigers, snakes, spiders, and birds. All of our early predators rolled up into one. Therefore, in early civilizations, the younglings had to learn to not only face their fear of this creature but overcome it.

Luke now knows he must face this masked evil Darth Vader and that he must fight alongside the Rebellion as they take down the Death Star.

The cave may represent the center of the story and the terrible danger or an inner conflict which the Hero must face. Whether it be facing his greatest fear or most deadly foe, the Hero must draw upon everything he has learned along his journey to climb the obstacle in front of him. This is the ultimate showdown. If the Hero fails, he with either die or life will never be the same.

Sticking solely to Lucas's first film in the original trilogy, as he would literally have Luke go into a cave and face his Shadow in a later movie, the Death Star--a weapon that has the ability to destroy planets--becomes the cave and Darth Vader the dragon.

"The ultimate dragon is within you…" -Joseph Campbell

One of the things that people don't tell you about when you are young is that simply to live is difficult. I am not making excuses or levying the weight of your shoulders, I am merely telling you here and now, that you're going to carry that weight your whole life.

However, Campbell succinctly stated the secret to it all, "Follow your bliss." Find your purpose, listen to the muses, and go on your adventure and this weight suddenly seems more bearable. Why? Because you have meaning.

Goals give man focus. The New England Patriots could never win six championships (and counting) over the span of two decades if they did not have clear goals.

The NFL is hard. Injuries, trades, and the sheer madness of the season from the press to the game itself make a child's game a big deal. Life is hard. If football was just another metaphor and we were to extrapolate meaning out of it the way Campbell did with myths, we suddenly see that trials and tribulations await us all. The only way you can live up to the challenge and not fall under the weight of your adventure is by finding your bliss and seeing your journey through to the end.

"It is by going down into the abyss that we recover the treasures of life. Where you stumble, there lies your treasure." -Joseph Campbell

The lesson and the return home.

"The privilege of a lifetime is being who you are." -Joseph Campbell

The enemy is now defeated. The Hero has survived or perhaps resurrected, but he has most definitely been changed. Whether it was an internal struggle or and physical test, the Hero emerges from battle stronger with a life lesson or a symbolic prize.

The reward is often a sacred object or greater knowledge. The treasure, however, is not the important end, as Hitchcock pointed out with his now infamous "McGuffin," and it is the change in the Hero that matters most. Their journey is not over though, as the Hero must return home with this new Elixir or knowledge.

Luke is saved from Vader by Han. Using the Force, Luke then destroys the Death Star. For now, the Rebellion has won.

"The goal of life is to make your heartbeat match the beat of the universe, to match your nature with Nature." -Joseph Campbell

Congratulations, you have completed the journey of this chapter! What is your sacred elixir? Well, I would be a fool to try and write it better than Campbell himself:

"Centuries of husbandry, decades of diligent culling, the work of numerous hearts and hands, have gone into the hackling, sorting, and spinning of this tightly twisted yarn. Furthermore, we have not even to risk the adventure alone; for the heroes of all time have gone before us; the labyrinth is thoroughly known; we have only to follow the thread of the hero-path. And where we had thought to find an abomination, we shall find a god; where we had thought to slay another, we shall slay ourselves; where we had thought to travel outward, we shall come to the center of our own existence; and where we had thought to be alone, we shall be with all the world."

Actionable Steps:

-Journal prompt: If you were the hero of your own movie, what would the story look like? Write a movie pitch. What is your Ordinary World? What are you secretly long to do? Who could be your mentors? What obstacles will you face? What Shadow stands in your way? What are you afraid to do? And, where must you journey to find the answers?

Day 4: Do

"If you can't fly, then run. If you can't run, then walk. If you can't walk, then crawl, but by all means, keep moving." - Martin Luther King Jr.

Life is a journey, and all journeys begin with a single step. Often, we let fear control our choices. We are afraid to even get started, because, if we do, what then? What if we're not read? Let me tell you, you never are. Life is meant for the living. So, get busy living, or get busy dying. What is one thing you have been afraid to try? Where is somewhere you have always wanted to visit? If you had total freedom, what would you do with your time? Find an answer to one of these questions, and then find a way to do it. Want to travel to Italy but don't have the time or the funds, then go to an Italians restaurant and order a nice bottle of wine. Want to write a screenplay, but don't know where to start, then watch a documentary about filmmaking and see how other people did it. Take a baby step towards your goal. Align yourself with where you want to be and do something, even if it is as simple as sipping a martini shaken, not stirred.

Chapter 3:

"If you aim at nothing, you will hit it every time." - Zig Ziglar

Set your goals.

It has been repeated by a thousand other authors, but it deserves to be repeated again. There is no more practical advice on this planet than goal setting.

I'll be honest. I hated this phrase for the longest time. In high school, I couldn't stand when "motivational speakers" came to school. In college, I hated, even more, the men and women who paraded around like charlatan's touting "how to succeed" after college, or the "secrets to making money."

Because of this animosity for success buzzwords and jolly jargon, I steered away from many of the speakers, authors, and figures who could mentor me best.

Hilary Hinton "Zig" Ziglar was a charming American author, salesman, and motivational speaker originally from Coffee County, Alabama. Author of fifteen books and countless seminars, Zig was the quintessential motivational speaker.

Funny with a voice like molasses, Zig always had a quip handy and a story ready; however, what he was most famous for was his advocacy of setting goals.

"Lack of direction, not lack of time, is the problem. We all have twenty-four-hour days."
-Zig Ziglar

Listed below is a summation and exemplification of Zig's seven-step process for setting clear, precise goals.

Why are we starting here? Because, if you don't know where you are going, how will you know when you get there?

Before we continue, two quick notes:
1) Write it down, and 2) Give yourself time.

"You don't have to be great at something to start, but you have to start to be great at something." -Zig Ziglar

Step 1: State the Goal

What do you want? Whatever it is, write it down. Write it down on a little piece of paper and carry it around with you. Write it on your wall. Write it on your whiteboard. Take a picture of it and save it as the background on your phone.

Whatever you do, make sure that you get crystal clear about what your goals are and where you are heading.

"Outstanding people have one thing in common: An absolute sense of mission." -Zig Ziglar

Bruce Lee said, "A goal is not always meant to be reached, it often serves simply as something to aim at." Sometimes, the thing we set out to achieve is not where we end up, however, it is the journey that changes us.

Step 2: Set a Deadline

Football has four quarters. Baseball has nine innings. Hockey has three periods, and no one really understands why. The point is, everything has a deadline. Sports, movies, books, they all have an ending in mind. Set yours.
Step 3: Identify the Obstacles

"Sometimes adversity is what you need to face to become successful" - Zig Ziglar

If you were the hero of your own movie, then guess what? You are going to face challenges. Read any book on screenwriting like "Save the Cat" by Blake Snyder or "Story" by Robert McKee and do you know what the one thing they all have in common is? Characters must face obstacles. Therefore, how is your life any different? The great power you have in your hand, however, is imagination. You can imagine what the challenges are going to be that you are going to face. So, write down what you believe the walls are going to be standing in your way.

But guess what? There are going to be some unforeseen tests. There will be trials you did not see coming. And just like a novel or a movie, there is an answer to that too: your supporting cast.

Step 4: Identify the People, Groups, and Organizations that Can Assist

There is the great American myth of the "Self-Made Man." He did it alone. He went out into the wilderness and survived. Then, he came back with a treasure that saved the world.

I am here to tell you now, no one does it alone. Novelists need publishers. Screenwriters need directors. Ballplayers need coaches. Furthermore, we all need help in one way or another.

"You will get all you want in life, if you help enough other people get what they want." - Zig Ziglar

No matter how many times the media says that Michael Jordan was the greatest basketball player of all time, or that Tom Brady is the G.O.A.T., or that the Hammer of God Mariano Rivera was the best closer, we must all remember one simple thing: it was a team. Jordan didn't win anything before Phil Jackson and Scottie Pippen, not to mention there were three other players on the court. Brady would have a difficult time hitting his receivers without a powerful offensive line and a brilliant head coach, and Rivera would never have wrapped up so many games if his team hadn't of put him there in the first place.

Step 5: List the Benefits of Achieving the Goal

What happens when you reach the mountain top? Is there a trophy? Money? Power?

The road is going to be hard. Nothing worth attaining is easy. When times get tough, the first thing to falter is your sense of mission. The first question you are going to ask yourself is, "Why am I doing all this?"

"What you get by achieving your goals is not as important as what you become by achieving your goals." -Zig Ziglar

One of the greatest things we can do to dig deeper is to hold on to our childlike curiosity and ask, "Why?" Why do I want this? Why do I do this? Why is this so important to me? We are becoming mentally stronger, which means, we must ask ourselves questions other people are not willing to face.

Step 6: List the Skills You Need to Acquire to Attain the Goal

No one was born with a complete toolkit. Lebron James may be the most complete basketball player that has ever played the game. He is tall, strong, and mentally fit to lead his team; however, he didn't start out that way.

He may have been blessed with height, but to be the player he wanted to be he had to learn how to shoot, how to lead, and how to be the player his teammates needed him to be.

If Lebron James has to work every day to get better, then what do you think you should be doing?

"FEAR has two meanings: 'Forget Everything And Run' or 'Face Everything And Rise.' The choice is yours." -Zig Ziglar

This is another common theme we see in novels. The hero makes the choice to pursue adventure. Yet, the person he is at the start of his journey is not the person who can attain the prize. Luke Skywalker is not ready to be a Jedi at the start of *Star Wars*, he lacks the knowledge and skills. Frodo Baggins not only needs allies, but he must discover the strength to carry the ring to Mount Doom.

Step 7: Develop a Plan

The final step, based on the knowledge you have gathered, what is your best course of action?

I am not asking you to be a chess grandmaster and layout 261 scenarios from your opening move. This is not Go.

After asking yourself the previous questions, what is the first step you should take? There is a saying in improv, "Bring a brick." What it means is that it is up to the improv performer to bring an idea, bring the first step. Where do we start? Then, allow imagination and ingenuity to take hold.

"People often say that motivation doesn't last. Well, neither does bathing - that's why we recommend it daily." -Zig Ziglar

So often, we become afraid of the sheer size of the project. "I cannot write a book," we say to ourselves, or, "I could never lift 400 lbs." And it is true. At this moment, you cannot write a book. You cannot lift 400 lbs. It takes time. It takes practice. It takes a plan.

A novelist can only tackle one chapter, one paragraph, one sentence at a time. A lifter can only lift what his body is capable of lifting today, and then, tomorrow, he will return and lift what his body is capable of lifting.

Mike Tyson has a great quote about plans, "Everybody has a plan until they get punched in the mouth." Does this mean we should abandon all forward thinking and improvise the entire journey? No.

Tyson was a fury of force in the boxing ring, and he planned to be so tenacious, so violent that his opponent's plan could not take hold. He imposed his will on his opponent.

The point is that the best-laid plans go awry. Nothing works the way it is supposed to. This does not mean we do not plan, it merely says that we plan and make decisions to the best of our knowledge, and then, when the moment comes, we must "be like water" as Bruce Lee would say and adapt to our surroundings.

Set your goal, make a plan, and take action.

Day 6: Dream

"A dream doesn't become reality through magic; it takes sweat, determination, and hard work." - Colin Powell

Perhaps we get the idea of Harry Potter magic ingrained in our heads as children because the world seems sun unexplainable. As we grow older and the tinge of what was vibrant wanes, we lose interest in such fairy tales. Suddenly, life seems hard and the road seems long. Yet we forget that what was once deemed magic is today commonplace. Magic is simply knowledge yet uncovered. What would an iPhone look like to a villager during the Dark Ages? All of these things, as real as they are today, were once ideas. They were once dreams. What are your biggest dreams? If no one ever found out, and trust me most of the world doesn't give a damn, what would you ask the world for? What is your biggest dream? How can you make that dream a reality? Has someone else accomplished it? Pay attention to your interests and your heroes, they are the guiding light to your inner self.

Chapter 4:

"If the challenge we face doesn't scare us, then it's probably not that important." Tim Ferriss

Write it down.

Successful people keep journals. Marcus Aurelius' notes to himself have become one of the greatest books on personal philosophy ever written. The quintessential American Benjamin Franklin put pen to paper so often that we praise everything from Silence Dogood to his personal ledger.

Journaling is one of the most powerful tools available to man, and yet, so many people leave it on the cutting room floor. Why?

"What do I write about?" people ask, or, "I don't have anything important to say." This is not about publishing the next great American novel or living up to the expectations of Tom Wolfe. Journaling is about digging deeper and discovering who you are.

Why write?

Until they develop an app that syncs your brainwaves with a psychologist personally developed for you by top coders in

Silicon Valley, pen and paper are the best tools we have for carving out our mind.

Next to reading, there is no more powerful tool for honing your thoughts.

Yet, we revere great authors like Maya Angelou and Ernest Hemingway so much that we compare ourselves to them, and as a great man once noted, "comparison is the thief of joy." Imagine if your trainer at the gym set you up to run a 40-yard dash, but then to "inspire you' Usain Bolt walked up next to you. Do you think you would beat the World's Fastest Man?

No. He would leave you in the dust, but when we train in the gym or on the page we are not lifting and running to compete in the next Olympics, we are putting in the time to make ourselves better.

I believe that people are afraid of writing, not because of what they might find, but of a similar fear of public speaking. It is a fear of judgment, yet, what is critical is that it is self-judgment.

"What we fear doing most is usually what we most need to do." -- Tim Ferriss

It is a false ideal people carry around with them that great authors, playwrights, and novelists sit down at a keyboard and suddenly become Mozart, that they are some sort of savant capable to turning laptop keys into piano strokes and outcomes Chopin without any prep work or sheet music.

Then, when we try and do the same, we find that our minds stumble, stall, and only don't produce the eloquent truth we "know" we possess.

Enter Timothy Ferris, author, podcaster, and life hacker. Listed as one of Fast Company 's "Most Innovative Business People," he was an early-stage tech investor/advisor and the author of five bestsellers, most notably "The 4-Hour Workweek." He, perhaps, became more famous when he launched the Tim Ferris Show podcast, an interview style podcasts where Tim asked the brightest and best in the world how they do what they do, and became, as the Observer noted, "the Oprah of audio."

If you would like to dig deeper on Ferries, check out all five of his books and start from Episode 1 of his podcast, both give great examples for how to build your toughness and many of the people quoted in this book like David Goggins and Jocko Willink have appeared on the show; however, in the spirit of Ferris, in order to "do more with less" we are going to focus on one of his most powerful tools, the five minute journal.

Inspired by another author, Julia Cameron's "The Artist's Way" (a book you will find in your further reading section), Tim condensed her journals into quick hits to steady his "monkey mind."

Quoting Cameron, "Once we get those muddy, maddening, confusing thoughts [nebulous worries, jitters, and preoccupations] on the page, we face our day with clearer eyes."

In this way, writing is a tool that can and should be used. The point here is not to become a writer, but to make your mind stronger, clearer, and more productive. No one will ever read what you write here. The point is to clean your mind. In this way, the process is the point, the journey is the way.

"I don't journal to "be productive." I don't do it to find great ideas, or to put down prose I can later publish. The pages aren't intended for anyone but me."

So, what is it?

"People will choose unhappiness over uncertainty." — Timothy Ferriss

For Ferris and Cameron at large, they are trying to figure things out and caging their monkey mind. The point is to give ourselves a place to go, at the beginning of a day, and get in tune with ourselves. We can figure out our goals, set new ones, find nuances in our lives, note important events, discover stories, remember jokes, establish mental models, whatever. The point is not to be witty, intelligent, or smart. We are not writing so that one day a Harvard grad student can write a dissertation on our notebooks. Hell, if Shakespeare had known what his plays would have become, he may not have had the strength to write Richard III.

Secondly, your journal is not a psychiatrist. It is not meant to solve anything. It is intended to materialize your thoughts and ideas so that you can see it on the page. Screenwriters talk about, "getting the bones down" to start a screenplay and get the ball rolling. Hereto, we are writing down our bones, so we can, potentially, pick them clean.

Even if it results in your bitching about your day, the thought is now on paper and doesn't have to eat away at you for the next 24-hours.

"Focus on being productive instead of busy." - Tim Ferris

Actionable Steps:

-Every morning for the next 26 days, write for Five minutes when you first wake up. There are two ways to approach the journal. First, set aside five minutes to write stream of conscious on anything that comes to mind. If you find you want to keep writing, go for it.

Two, if you are foggy, in a hurry, or simply lack the strength to pull a topic or two out of thin air, use the following prompts to spur your answers. In this method, we will focus on gratitude, interests, the spark in our everyday lives, affirmations, and goals.

1) *I am grateful for...x 3*
2) *Today would be awesome if…*
3) *One story worthy moment from yesterday was…*
4) *I am…x3*
5) *If I only accomplish one thing today it is...*

-Make sure you wake up early enough to get this in. The point here is building a habit and giving yourself time.

-Oversleep? Running late? Don't worry. Settle in when you get a chance and knock it out. We are building a new routine for your brain. One cookie doesn't break your diet but eating the whole bag will. If you miss a morning don't miss a month.

"Conditions are never perfect. 'Someday' is a disease that will take your dreams to the grave with you." Tim Ferriss

Day 8: Write

"The first draft is just you telling yourself a story" - Terry Pratchett

Write down your thoughts. Write down your ideas. Write down the fleeting moments of your life when the moon lights the way. Start your journal, even if it is just one paragraph at a time. There is nothing more powerful than seeing your thoughts become reality, be it in the form of a story, an essay, or just random thoughts about pop culture. There is no need to publish this, you are not writing for an audience. You are writing for yourself.

Chapter 5:

"True will power. I'm going to (expletive) fail, I'm going to (expletive) fail, I'm going to (expletive) fail, and I will succeed." – David Goggins

You are going to fail.

To accomplish anything, we must first learn, not only to fail but to learn from our failures.

Jordan was cut from his high school basketball team, Walt Disney was fired for lacking imagination, Elvis Presley, Lucille Ball, and Carol Burnett were all told to pack it in and go home due to their "astounding" lack of talent.

And yet, their names live on, their doubters do not (after all, Teddy Roosevelt reminds us that it is "The man in the arena" that matters most).

First and foremost, failure is a chance to learn. The Great Bambino Babe Ruth once said, "Every strike brings me closer to my next home run."

By now someone has quoted Thomas Edison's line to you. If not, here's Nicholas Cage's version from National Treasure, "You know, Thomas Edison tried and failed nearly 2,000 times to develop the carbonized cotton-thread filament for the incandescent light bulb...And when asked about it, he said "I didn't fail; I found out 2,000 ways how not to make a light bulb," but he only needed one way to make it work."

Right next to the Great One Wayne Gretzky's "You miss 100 of the shots you don't take," and Jordan's, "I've missed more than 9,000 shots in my career. I've lost almost 300 games. Twenty-six times I've been trusted to take the game-winning shot and missed. I've failed over and over and over again in my life. And that is why I succeed."

Yet, I believe we can do better than an inspirational office poster hanging behind your boss's desk. A cliché may be something that at one time was true, but it has been so beaten to death that even flies won't touch it.

Enter David Goggins.

"You're gonna fail, you're gonna be in your head, and you're gonna be saying I'm not good enough. It's about how you overcome that." **– David Goggins**

Goggins knows failure. Why? Because he has taken all the shots, he has burned every filament and burst every light bulb.

Goggins is a retired Navy SEAL and someone who will be referenced in this book a lot. He is the only member of the

U.S. Armed Forces to complete SEAL training (including two Hell Weeks), the U.S. Army Ranger School (where he graduated as Enlisted Honor Man) and Air Force Tactical Air Controller training.

Goggins is an accomplished man. At one time he held the Guinness World Record for pull-ups (4,030 in 17 hours). As an endurance athlete, Goggins has completed over 60 ultra-marathons, triathlons, and ultra-triathlons, regularly finishing in the top-five and setting course records along the way.

Yet, he was not always the accomplished man he is today.

In the late 1990s, after spending four years in the Air Force, Goggins weighed almost 300 pounds. He was told then that he was too heavy to make it through SEAL training. In less than three months, he returned weighing 190 pounds.

If you were to ask Goggins or read his phenomenal books on mental toughness, he would be the first person to tell you all of the awards, medals, accolades and magazine articles don't mean a hill of beans. It's not what he's after.

"It's so easy to be great nowadays because everyone else is weak. If you have ANY mental toughness, if you have any fraction of self-discipline; The ability to not want to do it, but still do it; If you can get through to doing things that you hate to do: on the other side is GREATNESS" – David Goggins Quotes

He's not trying to be number one in the world. He's not interested in how many races he's run. He doesn't keep track of the miles he's gone. There's no scoreboard.

For Goggins, it's about pushing himself day in and day out. It's about choosing to test yourself, about putting obstacles in front of yourself. It's about running the hardest races and most challenging military tests to see what he's made of. The suffering, the sweat, and the sacrifice are all part of the journey of self-discovery.

"At the end of the day, hard work may not be enough. You still may fail. But you keep going out there and go after it." – David Goggins

Another military man and infamous failure, Sir Winston Churchill, would share a similar sentiment in his time, "Success is the ability to go from failure to failure without losing your enthusiasm."

The point to all of this is that every hero fails. We live in a time where people share their highlight reels with us every day on Instagram. The celluloid dream of Hollywood has reached into our homes and given everyone the right to be their own public relations manager.

What we don't see is how many times Conor McGregor got knocked down before he learned to fight. What we don't understand are the countless snaps Tom Brady and the Belichick's Patriots took before coming together in 2000.

Why do we fall down? So, we can learn to pick ourselves back up.

Learn to take your blows.

"A warrior is a guy that goes 'I'm here again today. I'll be here again tomorrow and the next day.' It's a person who puts no limit on what's possible." – David Goggins

Actionable Steps:

-Start today. Whatever the thing is, start today. Want to write a book? Write the outline. Want to gain muscle? Join the gym. Take the first step towards the new you. Why? Because you are going to fail, and the sooner you start failing, the faster you can start improving.

Day 10: Suck

"Failure isn't fatal, but failure to change might be" - John Wooden

Dare to suck. Dare to do something outside your boundaries. Great fighters seek out the real challenge. Jiu-Jitsu rollers do not look to beat the white belt, but instead, find the challenge their heart pumping and the mind racing. How much of life do we miss out on by staying in our lane? We are all still that kid afraid to upset his peers. Well, not today. What is something you find fascinating? What is something that terrifies you? Have you always wanted to learn fencing? How about dance, or sing? Find a place to wing it and scare the shit out of yourself. Do something that reminds you that you are alive and that you truly can do anything you want.

Chapter 6:

*"Relaxation happens only when allowed, not as a result of 'trying' or 'making.'" - **Timothy Gallwey***

There is nothing quite like being in the zone. As kids, we all envisioned ourselves in the moment: bottom of the ninth, no time left on the clock, fourth and goal from the one, down by two, and game on the line. Time slows down. The crowd holds their breath. A hush enters the arena.

Sports brings out the best in us. It gives us a focus and an escape. It begs the best of us. It raises our hopes, crushes our dreams, and unites people across political lines.

It also requires a level of mental mastery beyond that of everyday life. To throw a perfect game, hit for eagle, or sink a free throw is as much mental as it is physical. Add to the task a screaming crowd of thousands of fans, cameras, and the possibility of living in infamy on the internet, and you've got a jackpot of anxiety.

The game is hard, and it requires hours upon hours to be competent, let alone good. One of the big changes in sports over the last decade is the focus on mental training.

Meditation is a buzzword today. Gurus have hopped on the mindfulness train, and for a good reason. Yet, if pictures of cozy mugs and palm facing upwards are not your cup of tea, then how can you use this practical discipline?

What I hope to offer you in this chapter is another tool, minus the B.S. I do not mean to attack ancient traditions or impede upon practice, but sometimes the yoga retreat and incense can turn off the importance of the exercise.

With that in mind, why meditate?

The practice offers increased happiness and patience. It lowers levels of stress and depression. It gives us a tool to deal with anxiety and ultimately provides us with a way to discipline our mind.

Meditation is about training your mind, plain and simple. It is about developing focus and awareness and developing a sense of perspective. It's about observing your thoughts and feelings and creating space so that you can see how your mind works and understand yourself better.

Similarly, mindfulness, a sort of brother to meditation, is centering on the present and being fully engaged in the moment.

By becoming more aware, we can better understand the connection between our thoughts and how those thoughts arise.

We live in an age of instant access. With the swipe of a finger, we can be whisked away to a developing empire, check in with friends across the country, or be bombarded with news from around the world. It's easy to be entertained to the point of vegetation. Disconnecting with the world around us is easy.

It is a practice and experience. It is a way to cultivate awareness and get in touch with who we are and discover clarity, compassion, and, dare I say it, peace. By doing this, we learn to live in the moment and accept our "monkey mind."

In this way, our morning journal becomes a meditation, as does our 5k or our time in the gym. It is not solely about sitting quietly in a serene space with water trickling down the walls. Meditation can be done anywhere, anytime, eyes open or closed.

We are not striving to be Buddhist monks, yogis, or Jedi masters.

If your goal is to fly off and train with Tibetan monks, then, by all means, leave on that jet plane. If, however, you have other goals in mind, then the practice offered here is to give you another tool to develop mental clarity and toughness.

In fact, if you want to see the power of concentration and the benefit of moving meditations look no farther than the TV.

Athletes are prime examples of people who have developed a practical meditation within their sports. There has been no more exceptional book written on this than Timothy Gallwey's "The Inner Game of Tennis."

*"It is said that in breathing man recapitulates the rhythm of the universe. When the mind is fastened to the rhythm of breathing, it tends to become absorbed and calm." - **Timothy Gallwey***

Here, we switch the metaphors. In meditation, the practice is to focus on the breath. In tennis, the practice is to focus on a little, brightly colored ball that just so happens to be moving at extreme speeds. In both cases, who or what is the enemy? Is it the opponent? Is it the crowd? Is it the ball or the breath?

None of them. Ultimately, the enemy is yourself. We compete with who we were the day before to get better, but too often, we treat ourselves like an enemy and not an ally.

We beat ourselves up with shameful self-talk and comments to our psyche that would make our mother's blush. As Gallwey notes, athletes must learn to relax these useless thoughts. Perhaps being hard on yourself works when you are training and not settling for less, but in the moment, when the game is on, you must learn to let it ride.

"The player of the inner game comes to value the art of relaxed concentration above all other skills; he discovers a true basis for self-confidence; he learns that the secret to winning any game lies in not trying too hard."
-Timothy Gallwey

As in meditation, Gallwey preaches the idea of a "relaxed mind" approach to the game. In other words, an athlete cannot force the game to come to them, they must let it flow. Or, as the more notable Jedi master Yoda once said, "A Jedi's strength flows through the Force."

Flow is the ultimate goal. We cannot force other people's will to bend to our own, that is the way of the Dark side. Instead, we must learn to work in congruence with our thoughts. We must train our brains to relax and accept the moment, rather than fighting for a past that does not exist and a future made up only of ideals.

In sport and in meditation, we seek a relaxed concentration. This, as Gallwey notes, is the supreme art because nothing can be achieved without it. Whether we call it the flow state, in the zone, or on fire, we have all experienced that feeling of effortless excellence. A sport like tennis gives us the physical ability to develop this skill. A practice like meditation gives us the intellectual discipline to develop it. To learn this art, practice is needed, and the beauty of this practice is that concentration, flow, and mindfulness can be practiced at any time, anywhere.

*"The development of inner skills is required, but it is interesting to note that if, while learning tennis, you begin to learn how to focus your attention and how to trust in yourself, you have learned something far more valuable than how to hit a forceful backhand." - **Timothy Gallwey**️*

Actionable Steps:

-What sort of game do you play? Do you passively compete, over analyze, or beat yourself up when you play? We often take away the joy from the games we loved as children. Find that game and play it again, however, while you play take note of the conversation going on in your head.

A Simple Meditative Practice:
  - *Find a quiet place*
  - *Set aside 3-5 minutes*

1. *Find a comfortable spot. This can be standing, sitting, or lying down. Whatever works for you.*
2. *Set your timer*
3. *Close your eyes*
4. *Observe your breath*
5. *Take notice of your body*
6. *Take note of your thoughts. Observe them, but do not engage with them*
7. *Take in your practice*
8. *Repeat every day, or when needed*

Day 12:

"Listening is an art that requires attention over talent, spirit over ego, others over self."
Dean Jackson

Instagram gives us a voice. Facebook gives us a platform. YouTube gives us an outlet. In today's world, everyone's talking and nobody's listening. It seems like everyone is just waiting for their turn to speak, rather than opening their minds. Today's task is to listen. Call a friend, set up a date for drinks, or start a conversation with a random stranger, but listen to them intently. Give them your full attention. Do not check your phone. Do not interrupt. Let them speak and give them your focus. Meditation is a practice that applies to more than just breathing and stretching.

Chapter 7:

This chapter is not full of quotes or inspiration.

This is perhaps the simplest tool of the whole book: The Five Whys.

Created by the Toyota Motor Corporation to aid in problem-solving, The Five Why Method is precisely what it sounds like. When problem-solving, continue asking yourself why until you reach the core issue.

Taiichi Ohno, the originator of the System and author of "The Toyota Production System", encouraged his company to dig at a problem until they found the root cause.

This childlike approach delivers massive results. Children are naturally curious. They are born scientists. They want to understand how and why things work the way they do.

Then, somewhere in our youth, that curiosity is beaten out of us. We are told to sit down, shut up, and listen. Do as we are told. Follow directions. Do not think outside the box.

So, when the child is one day asked to lead, often, we lack the requisite skills to self-analyze because all we have done our whole lives is follow instructions.

We are building mental models, methods of challenging and handling challenges. The Five Why Method allows us to dissect our performance and failures in a constructive way to decipher what went awry.

When we fail, face an obstacle, or just want to understand a belief or value, it is best to look at the concept with a methodical approach.

The first why is simple, "Why did 'X' happen?" Usually, the answer presents itself rather quickly, and efficiently. Humans are good at pointing fingers and assessing blame. Even the second and third layers can appear rapidly; however, the fourth and fifth levels usually bring the most results as we are reaching a deeper level of critical thinking.

For us, the first why is also in line with Simon Sinek's TED talk, which is, our purpose. Why we do what we do is more important than what we do. In the larger picture, whatever your journey, ask yourself why you do this thing. We often find ourselves herded into careers and paths that are not our own. What are you attracted to? What are you interested in? Where do you see duct-tape?

It is best to do this exercise, as opposed to explaining it. Here are the steps to completing Toyota's method:

1. Identify the Problem
2. Ask Why Five Times
3. Find solutions to the root cause

Therefore, what is a problem you currently face?

Why is it a problem?

Why is that?

Why is that?

Why is that?

Why is that?

If this is the root cause, how do we solve this problem?

In our case, we are wanting to build mental toughness. Therefore, our initial problem may be along the lines of, "I lack the courage to make difficult decisions."

Why? "I am afraid of the answers that I may find."

Why? "Because these answers may result in me having to make difficult changes in my life, I am not comfortable with."

Why? "While I have not accomplished my goals, I am comfortable. I have mild success and life well. If I push, I may have to give that up."

Why? "Because, despite accomplishing some of my goals, I have not accomplished them all, and, in fact, I am still chasing the big fish. In order to catch it, I have let go of all the things that have gotten me this far."

Why? "Because deep down I know that this mild success is a mirage, a way to tell myself it is okay, I made it this far. If I want what I say I want, then I must keep pushing."

Now, how do we solve the problem at hand? In this example, a question of "fear" leads to a deepen answer of "purpose." The fear to make tough decisions was a way of hiding. It is now time to address the issue. How do we correct the course? How do we build upon this knowledge?

While the example was psychological, the method can be quite practical. It can be used on issues of teams and sports, as well as methods and practices.

Actionable Steps:

-What is a problem you currently face?
-Ask yourself why five times.
-What can you do to change it?

Day 14: Learn

"Live as if you will die tomorrow. Learn as if you will live forever." - Gandhi

The spirit of asking questions is learning. In school, too often the ability to question is driven out of us. Today we have access to an infinite Library at Alexandria. Seek out something you don't understand, be it quantum mechanics or how to style your hair properly. What is something you have always wondered about? Don't know who the Knight Templars are? What happened to the Arc of the Covenant? Spark mystery in your life by digging at questions that bring excitement.

Chapter 8:

"The purpose of life is finding the largest burden that you can bear and bearing it." - *Jordan B. Peterson*

The Beatles have a powerfully simple song called "Carry that Weight." It's only three stanzas long with several interludes, but in essence, it is such a powerful song. Sandwiched between "Golden Slumbers" and "The End," "Carry that Weight" is the kind of song that inexplicably lingers long after you've turned your record player off.

Listen to one of Dr. Jordan B. Peterson's lectures or interviews for more than five minutes, and you will inevitably feel the same way, along with wondering what the "The Gulag Archipelago," is and attempting to grasp the gravitas of *Pinocchio.*

In the media, Dr. Peterson is portrayed as a controversial figure, landing himself right in the middle of the culture wars, but spend time digging into his material and you quickly realize his message is one of meaning.

"I don't think that you have any insight whatsoever into your capacity for good until you have some well-developed insight into your capacity for evil." — Jordan B. Peterson

Dr. Peterson is a professor of psychology at the University of Toronto, however, in his lifetime he has been a dishwasher, gas jockey, bartender, short-order cook, beekeeper, oil derrick bit re-tipper, plywood mill laborer, and railway line worker.

"Face the demands of life voluntarily. Respond to a challenge, instead of bracing for catastrophe." – Jordan B. Peterson

The man of internet acclaim for touting the hierarchical significance of crabs and why every human should read Tolstoy and Nietzsche, Peterson is a sort of modern moral philosopher.

His book original lecture series/textbook "Maps of Meaning" lay out the power of his intellect. After rising to internet acclaim, his follow up the book "12 Rules for Life," build upon his fame of being a pragmatist; however, he rose to internet fame after several lectures and interviews went viral launching him into the current intellectual circle.

If you want to dig deeper into the lessons Dr. Peterson has to offer, I highly recommend his books, which are, like he refers to Nietzsche, "a series of bombs."

Like the Beatles, his lessons are simple, yet profound. They are the kind of things that if they came from our father or mother, we would dismiss as dated and cliché. Yet, with Dr. Peterson, he brings with him years of study and wit that rivals the authors he pulls from.

He touts rules such as, "Make your bed," or, "Keep your house in order," and "Tell the truth." Yet, in the same breath, he will deliver a powerful insight that borders on the genius.

"Every bit of learning is a little death. Every bit of new information challenges a previous conception, forcing it to dissolve into chaos before it can be reborn as something better. Sometimes such deaths virtually destroy us."
— Jordan B. Peterson

So, what can a Canadian psychology professor teach us about mental toughness? Dr. Peterson is a slightly different teacher than the rest of the mentors in this book. His lessons are about man's suffering and the meaning we can discover within it. He is an antidote to a time analyzing itself on the internet and spreading untested ideas like a virus through social media.

He is a champion of wisdom and its practical use in modern society. He is a proponent of action and reflection, of living life and learning from it, not solely attempting to understand its meaning from an armchair.

"You don't get to choose not to pay the price, you only get to choose which price you pay"
— Jordan B. Peterson

Life is for the living, and yet, so many have lived before us. What lessons can we learn from them? What timeless wisdom has man deemed worthy to be handed down through the ages in the form of myth, story, and knowledge?

In all his media, Dr. Peterson believes in the power of story. He believes in the significance of myth and narrative to help humans process difficult information.

In drama, playwrights and actors learn the significance of choice. Actors are told a character is all about choices. What does your character do? Not what do they talk about doing or what they philosophize doing, but what do they actually do? Playwrights and screenwriters craft their stories to hinge on the significance of a single choice, a choice that is heightened by the summation of all previous actions.

If you were the hero in your own play, what would be the actions you take? What is your sole aim, your super objective in life? What have you done to move towards your goal? What has hindered you? Have you stopped? Why? Is it a brief respite or have you given up hope? Has the weight of your burden grown too large?

In Chapter 2, we talked about Joseph Campbell's hero's journey, an integral part of Dr. Peterson's Jungian based psychological approach which discussions of the significance of metaphor. Campbell to understand the power of myth and the importance of the role of story in our lives. Stories allow us not only to project ourselves into the protagonist but also see our world reflected back. Therefore, when we watch something like Pinocchio or read something like "Lord of the Rings" we are able to ascertain more information than merely entertainment.

In every story from Superman to Hamlet, the character chooses to pick up the cross and bear it. They either become the hero we want them to be or fail to complete their journey.

In our own lives, we must recognize the power of choice and the responsibility of action. We must begin to put our house in order and take note of the way we treat others and ourselves. Too often, we allow life to throw us this way and that without taking stock. We love to "blame the refs" for our loss rather than take ownership of our failures.

It's time to be better. It's taking ownership of your own life and become mentally healthy in a way that mirrors the great lessons of history.

"You're going to pay a price for every bloody thing you do and everything you don't do. You don't get to choose to not pay a price. You get to choose which poison you're going to take. That's it." - Jordan B. Peterson

In a Quora post, Dr. Peterson listed 40 maxims for life. Here, I've boiled it down to mirror his second book.

Another 12 Rules from Jordan B. Peterson

1. Tell the Truth
2. Do not do things that you hate
3. Act so can tell the truth about how you act
4. Pursue what is meaningful, not what is expedient
5. Make one thing better every single place you go
6. Do not allow yourself to become arrogant or resentful
7. Treat yourself as if you are someone you are responsible for helping
8. Nothing well done is insignificant
9. Dress like the person you want to be
10. Read something by someone great
11. Remember that what you do not yet know is more important than what you already know
12. Be grateful in spite of your suffering

Actionable Steps:

-Journaling Prompt: What burden do you choose to bare? What price are you willing to pay for your goals? What is important to you?

-What great book have you always wanted to read? Start it alongside this Book.

-Make a list of your own 12 Rules for Life.

Day 16: Lift

"Just remember, somewhere, a little Chinese girl is warming up with your max." – Jim Conroy

Do you even lift bro? We all carry a metaphysical weight and sometimes there is no better way to shed that burden than by picking up heavy things and sitting them down. Today, move your body. If you don't work out, try a bodyweight routine. If you lift, do yoga. Do something, anything, that challenges and expands both your mind and your body. The two are not separate but intertwined. There is as much intellect in our fingers as there is in our cortex. If you want to build a stronger mind, start by building a stronger body.

Chapter 9:

"Mental toughness is going out there and doing what's best for the team – even though everything isn't going exactly the way you want it to." - Bill Belichick

For a while, Bill Belichick was in the running for the greatest head coach in professional football history. This year, 2019, the debate is over.

For the uninitiated, Belichick has led the New England Patriots of the National Football League (NFL) to six Super Bowl titles (2002, 2004, 2005, 2015, 2017, and 2019), which is the most for an NFL head coach. To dig a little deeper, Belichick has more Super Bowl appearances than any NFL franchise (the Steelers, Cowboys, and Broncos all are in second with 8 while Belichick has 9).

Now, after winning his sixth ring in two decades and dominating the AFC East year in and year out, the New England Patriots and head coach Belichick have come to define success.

Yet, for Belichick, the disgruntled mumbler at the microphone whose favorite quote is, "Do your job," success did not come quickly, or easily. It wasn't until he turned 39 that he led a football team onto the field, and even then, it ended in disaster; however, it is not failure that defines Belichick's life as we know him, it is winning.

"You get the job done or you don't." - Bill Belichick

Belichick served as an assistant coach for the Detroit Lions, the Denver Broncos, and, finally, the New York Jets where he coached under legend Bill Parcells. After winning two Super Bowls with Parcels, Belichick was hired as the Cleveland Browns head coach. There, he led the Browns to just one winning season in five years and was fired. Parcels welcomed him back to the Jets, where he was promoted to head coach upon Parcels retirement, however, he only kept the job for a day before he left for New England.

"There are no shortcuts to building a team each season. You build the foundation brick by brick." - Bill Belichick

Things didn't look much brighter in Boston. Going 5-11 in his first year and opening his second with an 0-2 record in 2001, the Evil Empire did not get rolling until Belichick united with a then-unknown quarterback named Tom Brady (we could write a separate chapter on Brady, but he has his own book and TB12 method). Since then, the two have dominated the NFL.

Belichick's goal is simple: win. Early in his career he learned to analyze film, scout players, and evaluate teams. As he grew into the coach he is today, he learned to infuse every level of his organization with the winning mindset he carries.

Belichick's desire to win, his work ethic, and his mindset are the things of Napoleon and Alexander the Great. Learning from his mentors, he took what worked and learned how to build the best system.

"He understood that the key to success, the secret to it, was the mastery of the grunt work, all the little details… the little things were not little things, because it was the accumulation of little things that made big things happen."—David Halberstam, The Education of a Coach

This is perhaps my favorite lesson from Belichick. He started out doing the grunt work. He volunteered to study film, something that would become his greatest strength. Long ago, when no one else saw the significance of analyzing film, Belichick mastered the skill.

He did something no one else wanted to do, was willing to do, and he made himself the best at it. This skill, the ability to analyze data and evaluate players, has become the sole skill which the Patriots base their success around, and it was grunt work.

He took his father's understanding of formations and schemes and applied it to analysis. He then took that skill and gave its results to a mentor. Belichick made himself part of a team and then dedicated his skill to the greater good.

Here are two other key takeaways from Belichick's career:

1. **Find your passion and build on your natural talents.**
2. **Winning is a habit that must be refined**

To say Belichick loves football is to say the Atlantic Ocean is damp. The man is a master tactician. To become an expert or master of what you do, you need to make a considerable investment of time and effort. You learn from experience, admittedly, but you also learn tremendously during the "downtime" of when you're not actively competing for what it is that you do.

Belichick's father was a coach, and he instilled in him a love for the game. Yet that love of the game as not enough to make Belichick a professional athlete, in fact, he was barely a passable college one. So, how did Belichick take that love for the game and build the most successful football franchise of all time? He learned from the best, did the grunt work, and built upon what he believed in.

"Every game is an important game for us. Doesn't matter what's the next week – who we play, whether it's a bye week, Thanksgiving, Christmas, Halloween, Columbus Day. We don't care. We're just trying to go out there and win a game." - Bill Belichick

Excellence is a habit. Hard work is a habit. Winning is a habit. There are those who practice until they get it right and those who practice until they can't get it wrong. Guess which one Belichick is?

"His philosophy from the beginning was 'No stone left unturned' and 'No envelope unpushed in order to win.' And the result of that was you are worked to exhaustion. But he never asked you to do anything he wasn't doing."—Rick Venturi

Therefore, Belichick set the example and led the way. He put in more hours than everyone else and built a habit of winning from the ground up. He pays attention to details and loves players who do the same. In fact, if you were to ask Belichick about his players, he would tell you they are not the most talented, or the most gifted, however, what he would say is they are the most dedicated, the most versatile, and the most fundamentally sound.

"I think that we'll continue to try to look at ourselves in the mirror and see where we can do a better job, maybe where we can improve the process. But I think the fundamentals of the process will remain the same." - Bill Belichick

Every sports coach from the dawn of time has shouted the words, "Practice the fundamentals." Alongside "defense wins championships," this phrase branded onto your brain from Little League to Varsity.

For Belichick, it may, in fact, be his mantra.

Football is Belichick's obsession and it is the game that drives the man's success. His mental toughness is built around his love for the game and it gives him the strength to do the job, however small, that needs to be done.

"No days off." -Bill Belichick

You have to be willing to put in the work. Mental toughness is as much about understanding who you are and what you are willing to sacrifice as it is about the ability and mental models to make difficult decisions.

One of the things Belichick is known for is the ability to know when to let a player go. There are players so identified with the Patriots brand that you can't go into a bar in Boston without seeing a photo of them hanging on the wall, and yet, Belichick does not let that stand in the way of the ultimate goal. He knows the aim; therefore, he knows what must be done to hit the target.

What are you willing to put in the time for? Life is tough. Your journey is hard. You have to be willing to climb the mountain to get to the top.

Actionable Steps:

-Whatever your goal is, look at the whole life. If you want to start a business, look at the grunt work involved, not just the rewards. If you want to be an actor, are you willing to audition, learn lines, and wait tables to get by? If you want to be a writer are you willing to put in the hours and hours of work, the editing, the plotting, the failures? If you want to start a business are you willing to see your idea die, develop it again, and again?

-What skills are overlooked in your area? What small habits build lasting success? What exercises build the habit of excellence?

-What is your greatest success? What is your greatest failure? Which did you learn more from?

Day 18: Small Circles

"The secret is that everything is always on the line. The more present we are at practice, the more present we will be in competition, in the boardroom, at the exam, the operating table, the big stage. If we have any hope of attaining excellence, let alone of showing what we've got under pressure, we have to be prepared by a lifestyle of reinforcement. Presence must be like breathing." - Josh Waitzkin

Josh Waitzkin's book "The Art of Learning" is a must read, just not today. His ultimate lesson that he passes on is that mastery is about smaller and smaller circles. The dilatant focuses on the broad strokes so that they can entertain people at parties with parlor tricks, but the master focuses on the minutia. Rather than loading up on new information today, take something you are already good at. If you are a badass in the gym, what could you do to get better? If you are an amazing public speaker, who could you learn from to be even better? How do you move from mediocre to master? The more competent and confident we are in what we know the greater our ability to command and endure. Find something you are great at and decide to master it.

Chapter 10:

"This is the lesson: never give in, never give in, never, never, never, never — in nothing, great or small, large or petty — never give in except to convictions of honor and good sense. Never yield to force; never yield to the apparently overwhelming might of the enemy." - Winston Churchill

There may not be a more quotable leader in the history of mankind than Winston Churchill. He could spit brilliant quips like, "The price of greatness is responsibility," and then turn around and burn a rival as he did when Lady Aster remarked, "Winston, if I were your wife, I'd put poison in your coffee," to which Churchill responded, "Nancy, if I were your husband I'd drink it."

Wit and humor aside, Churchill led England through one of the most challenging trials in human history. When the man said, "If you're going through hell, keep going," meant it.

Known as a soldier and a journalist, an elitist and a statesman, an orator, and author, he led a complicated life defending democracy during a time of tyranny.

"Courage is what it takes to stand up and speak, it's also what it takes to sit down and listen." -Winston Churchill

We could spend an entire book zeroing in on what made Churchill mentally strong. In fact, each decade of his life reads like a different part of a book series, whether it is his early years as a soldier and a journalist when he penned five novels by the age of 26, or the following decade of turning on the conservative party and leading the charge for social reform such as the eight-hour workday and public health insurance, or the two-part bestseller where he lead the spirit of Britain through its darkest hour against Adolf Hitler and the Nazis only to be outed as Prime Minister two years later and then returning to defend against the Iron Curtain.

Needless to say, Churchill lived a life of excellence. To keep this chapter in the spirit of the rest of this book and not turn into a love fest for one of the greatest political thinkers of the 20th century, I have broken down the lessons we can learn from Churchill into four parts:

- **Courage**
- **Education**
- **Adventure**
- **Confidence**

Churchill never gave up, and he never surrendered. He always stood up for what he believed in, not merely giving in to the tide of his party. His nickname, "The English Bulldog," suits him perfectly, reminding us of his backbone and no matter the size of the obstacle in front of him he did not back down.

"All the greatest things are simple, and many can be expressed in a single word: freedom; justice; honor; duty; mercy; hope." - Winston Churchill

Courage

Churchill's famous "We shall fight on the beaches" speech he delivered to Parliament on June 4, 1940, is the perfect example of the man's indisputable backbone. What people forget about this speech is that it follows one of the greatest military disasters during World War II, and, in essence, Churchill is preparing a nation for invasion.

Yet, the man did not falter. In a trying time, he becomes the hero England needed, and through oration delivered the words a people needed to hear.

"Courage is rightly esteemed the first of human qualities because it has been said, it is the quality which guarantees all others." - Winston Churchill

We will all be tested. We all find ourselves in a cave of despair seemingly with no way out. We must all learn to face our fears, however large or small. When threatened by danger it is not a man's duty to run, but to stand and face the enemy. For, if you meet it "properly, without flinching, you will reduce the danger by half."

Confidence

Churchill was infamously self-confident, bordering, on some descriptions, as vain. He believed himself destined for greatness, as he noted in letters home during his first war; however, this belief in himself guided his actions. Arguably, it was this unwavering belief that pushed Churchill to be the rock he would become during World War II. While I am not suggesting you download the latest Tony Robbins seminar, I am recommending that you develop confidence in yourself, your abilities, and your decisions. Put in the hours to be the best at what you do and build your confidence in results. Hard work builds confidence, confidence builds success.

"We have before us many, many long months of struggle and of suffering. You ask, what is our policy? I can say: It is to wage war, by sea, land, and air, with all our might and with all the strength that God can give us; to wage war against a monstrous tyranny, never surpassed in the dark, lamentable catalogue of human crime. That is our policy. You ask, what is our aim? I can answer in one word: It is victory, victory at all costs, victory in spite of all terror, victory, however long and hard the road may be; for without victory, there is no survival." -Winston Churchill

Education

We remember Churchill not only for his decisions but for his wit. His personality was as much a part of his charm, if not more, than his policy. His witticisms and insults became legendary living on beyond his age. He was erudite and eloquent and wrote numerous books throughout his lifetime. He believed in the written word, and he handcrafted his speeches to perfect his timing and flow. He used the power of language to connect with people to be it on the battlefield or next to the hearth at home. To do all of this, Churchill was an avid reader and educated himself on the topics that mattered most to him.

The point is we must be lifelong learners. We must continue to add to our toolkit and deepen our knowledge on the topics relevant to us. Through mastery and education, we can improve our impact and develop the skills and confidence necessary to be successful.

"To improve is to change, so to be perfect is to change often." -Winston Churchill

Adventure

His life was an adventure. He fought on the battlefields and in parliament. He traveled the world many times over and relished his experiences into stories and novels. His early experiences paved the way for his understanding of the world and made him the leader Britain needed.

We live in a time that can lull us to sleep. We can live life through a laptop and never experience the beauty around us. The world is full of uncharted territories, both intellectual and physical. Never let fear of the unknown deter you from living your life. Mentally strong people seek out challenges, they seek out obstacles that seem insurmountable, and they never pass the buck.

"Every day you may make progress. Every step may be fruitful. Yet there will stretch out before you an ever-lengthening, ever-ascending, ever-improving path. You know you will never get to the end of the journey. But this, so far from discouraging, only adds to the joy and glory of the climb." -Winston Churchill

Actionable Steps:

-What is something that has always frightened you? How can you face that fear directly and overcome it?
-What is something you are better at than most people? How can you dive deeper into that skill and become a master?
-What is a period or topic you have always wanted to study but have put off? Find a book, online course, or local class that offers the insights you wish to.
-Where do you want to go? Find a new adventure. If you can't afford it now, find something that you can. Discover a new restaurant, a book, a museum, that allows you to scratch that it and start setting aside the funds to go on that adventure.

Day 20: Grind

"It's not that I'm so smart, it's just that I stay with problems longer." - Albert Einstein

Things that take a long time deter us. Big books, long hikes, and relationships scare the shit out of people. Yet, if there is one superpower that separates overachievers from normal people, it is their ability to stay with things longer. Today, we are trying to churn our graduates faster offering two-year degrees and master's programs that can be done over a summer course. Is that mastery? We are in the binge generation. Why wait to watch the next episode next week when you could stay up until midnight tonight? Sometimes, things take time. That does not mean we shouldn't push ourselves to learn faster but callouses take time to build up. Start something that can't be done in a day. Find a puzzle with a thousand pieces or a book that could serve as a paperweight--might I recommend something by Tolstoy or Dumas if you are feeling adventurous. We should all plant trees that only our children will benefit from the shade.

Chapter 11:

"Discipline equals freedom" -Jocko Willink

There is a link between building mental strength and the military. Perhaps it is because the consequences are grave and the need for success dire.

It is no surprise then that a man such as Jocko Willink, author, podcaster, and former Navy SEAL, makes an appearance in this book. He saw extensive combat action during the Battle of Ramadi, leading SEAL Team Three's Task Unit Bruiser, and is the author of "Extreme Ownership: How US Navy Seals Lead and Win."

A Silver and Bronze Star recipient for his service during the Iraq War, Jocko is a master at developing both physical and mental strength. The idea behind his book, like Jocko, is simple yet effective. The idea of "Extreme Ownership" is that the leader is responsible for the success or failure of the team. Period.

Real leaders do not pass the buck. They do not shift blame or look for scapegoats. Failure of a teammate is a failure of leadership. Leaders, therefore, don't look for excuses, they find a way to win.

"Extreme ownership. Leaders must own everything in their world. There is no one else to blame." – Jocko Willink

Whether its Bill Belichick or Nick Saban, successful leaders do not make excuses, and their measuring stick is simple. Did they win?

When people's lives are at stake, failure is more than an "L." The key to great leadership is that it starts with the individual, be it the coach or a freshman, and spreads to each of the team members, that is why great coaches seem to embody the spirit of their team.

In his book and his podcast, Jocko is great at doling out timeless wisdom to strengthen your mind. He is a proponent of daily exercise, martial arts training, and pushing your mind and body to the limits. He does this, not as a way to punish his body, but as a way to master his own mind.

"When you think you can't take any more… guess what? You can – It's PROVEN by the stories of ORDINARY PEOPLE in war." – Jocko Willink

You must be the master of your own mind. As the stoics suggested, you can only control your thoughts and actions, not those of other people. You can't change whether or solve traffic, so don't waste your time bitching about them.

"People who are successful decide they are going to be successful. They make that choice. They decide to study hard. They decide to work hard. They decide to be the first person to get to work and the last to go home." – Jocko Willink

We do not rise to the occasion, we rise to the level of our training. We must enforce higher standards on ourselves. Once the poor performance is accepted, then it becomes the standard. We must teach ourselves to be a better day in and day out. If we are to lead others, we must set high standards for ourselves.

Self-discipline is as simple as waking up early and making your bed every damn day.

To better yourself, focus on one decision at a time. We just can't pull in multiple directions at once. To accomplish anything, we must set our goal and drive towards that end.

Like Zig Ziglar said, motivation doesn't last; therefore, you cannot rely on it. Become your own motivation by building habits. Learn from everyone. Idolize no one. You can learn from everyone, even if it is learning what not to do.

Focus on your goals and take daily action to move closer to them. Like Warren Buffet's compound interest, small steps become miles over time. But we must do the work. We must put in the hours. Jocko likes to say there are no weekends. Belichick has shouted, "No days off," at Super Bowl parades. The weights are not going to move themselves. The book isn't going to write itself. The work has to be put in.

"Everyone wants some magic pill—some life hack—that eliminates the need to do the work. But that does not exist." – Jocko Willink

Mental toughness does not come from sitting on the couch watching TV. The strength to make the tough decisions isn't developed by sipping martinis and buying a new toy. We escape through the delusions of Netflix. We build our ego up by protecting it from challenges.

To build true mental toughness we must push our mind and body to its limits. The only way we can do that is by chasing the biggest goal, baring the biggest burden, and taking on the biggest dragon we can find.

To do this, we must step outside our comfort zone and learn. Find a class, find a teacher, take up a new skill or hobby. Commit yourself to a new sport, be a part of a team, and accept your role as a student. All great leaders learned to lead from others and forged their will their tests.

Set standards for yourself and hold the line. Adopt the skills you need to become successful and get after it.

"The Darkness cannot extinguish your light. Your WILL. Your determination. No matter what is happening—no matter how hard the fight is. As long as you keep fighting—you win." – Jocko Willink

Actionable Steps:

-Before you go to bed tonight, ask yourself:
Who am I?
What have I learned today?
How have I progressed towards my goals?
How have I become smarter/stronger?

Day 22: Habit

"Chains of habit are too light to be felt until they are too heavy to be broken." - Warren Buffett

If Einstein coined the phrase, "compound interest" then Warren Buffet monetized it. Heed the advice of one of the richest men ever. Habits make lasting changes. Bad habits destroy people's lives, good habits raise them. Brushing your teeth every night is a good habit. Making your bed is a good habit. They are repeatable. They are doable. They are accomplishable tasks. Often, if we want to see what is wrong with our lives, we do not have to look farther than our own bedrooms. We want to tell the world what to do with its money and other people how to make their lives better, but we so often refuse to maintain order in our own home. Good habits breed more good habits. What is one habit you can add to your life right now that has not been mentioned in this book? Is your room dirty? Clean it. The kitchen sink is full? Empty it! Sometimes kicking ass in life is as simple as paying the bills on time.

Chapter 12:

"During the season, your team should be led with exuberance and excitement. You should live the journey. You should live it right. You should live it together. You should live it shared. You should try to make one another better. You should get on one another if somebody's not doing their part. You should hug one another when they are. You should be disappointed in a loss and exhilarated in a win. It's all about the journey." - Coach K

Three names define NCAA basketball: John Wooden, Pat Summitt, and Mike Krzyzewski. An extensive number of books have been written on Wooden and his process, Summit is the most successful basketball coach in NCAA history, and Coach K has the hardest name to spell in the game.

Thanks to his challenging to spell and equally hard to pronounce last night, the aforementioned Coach K is the head basketball coach at Duke University, a program that was it not for Coach K would be a law school in the shadow of its much larger counterpart the University of North Carolina. With five NCAA Championships, 12 Final Fours, 12 ACC regular season titles, and 14 ACC Tournament championships, only Wooden (10) has more titles to his name than Coach K.

"Confrontation simply means meeting the truth head-on." - Coach K

Coach K defines success for me. Yet, part of what defines his success is his ability to change as a basketball coach. He began his coaching career under the "my way or the highway" style of coach Bobby Knight, who is also successful but remembered as much for his antics as he was for his coaching. Yet over Coach K's career, he has learned to adapt to the changing tide of the game again and again. He consistently learns as much from his players as they do from him, and every year is a new process.

It is remarkable how Coach K redefines his team and his process everyone. You cannot point to one signature that defines his coaching career except adaptability. He built powerhouse Senior based organizations like those lead by Christian Laettner as well as star-studded freshman talents like current team based around Zion Williamson.

He has remarked about learning new ways to coach from great players like Lebron James and Chris Paul, leaders in the NBA who taught Coach K how to work with exceptionally talented players. He has altered his lifelong man-to-man defense style to match the team's physicality or protect certain players from wearing out (most notably the National Championship with Jahlil Okafor, a star center, in 2015).

"I try to see each new season as a new challenge because I have a new team to work with, new opponents to encounter, and often new ideas and theories to try." - Coach K

Furthermore, he has done it the right way. Countless Duke basketball players have gone on to be leaders, not only in the NBA, but in broadcasting, business, and communities. During Coach K's time, there have been no scandals, no suspensions, no hot takes. Coach K is a collected leader on and off the court.

Over his years he has had a graduation rate as high as 100%, even maintaining a higher graduation rate during the era of "One-and-Done" players, a tag given to players who only play one year in NCAA before going to the NBA, than other major universities.

In other words, the man is a leader. He is disciplined. He is value driven. He is mentally tough. He views basketball as a means to an end. He sees himself as a teacher who coaches basketball.

So, what is there to learn?

1. The Team is Stronger than One Person
2. Adapt or Die
3. Conviction

1. "You develop a team to achieve what one person cannot accomplish alone. All of us alone are weaker, by far than if all of us are together." - Coach K

As Coach K has noted, when you first assemble a group, they're not a team, they are a group of individuals. He understands the significance of the "Jim's and Joe's" as opposed to the "x's and o's." The importance of a team is the people assembled.

While we love the cult of personality, most actions cannot be done alone. Frodo needed Samwise a dwarf and an elf. Jordan needed Pippen, Kerr, and the Zen Master Coach Phil Jackson. The Avengers had to come together to defeat Loki, that strange robot Ultron, and Thanos. Hell, even in the NBA it took the greatest team ever assembled, The Golden State Warriors (under Steve Kerr mind you) to defeat the unbelievably talented Lebron James.

Leadership takes time. Trust takes time. Teams take time. No one, not even Coach K, begins with trust, it must be earned. It is this understanding that has led Coach K to be successful at multiple levels. He allows his team to take responsibility. He allows his players to develop into men.

In our lives, we operate in teams. We call them businesses, families, and friends, but we work in groups. Even if we play individuals sports like tennis and golf, we still need coaches and caddies. Also, if we produce solo music and dance, we still need producers and a beat.

I will write it here: Elon Musk did not do it alone. Jeff Bezos did not do it alone. Marky Mark needed the Funky Bunch.

You are the summation of the five people you spend the most time with. When you are building your team, ask yourself what this person brings to the table. Be it in the office or in life, we often saddle ourselves with people that do not have our best interests in mind. Often, people see us a means to an end. If you are genuinely trying to do something amazing, and you are, then you must protect your inner circle.

Note* We all have to deal with difficult people. It is a fact of life. While we can limit their impact on our experience, we cannot eradicate them entirely, whether it is the slacking coworker who is just there until happy hour, or the guy who cuts you off in 5 o'clock traffic. In this instance, I recommend Marcus Aurelius' quote:

> "Begin each day by telling yourself: Today I shall be meeting with interference, ingratitude, insolence, disloyalty, ill-will, and selfishness – all of them due to the offenders' ignorance of what is good or evil. But for my part I have long perceived the nature of good and its nobility, the nature of evil and its meanness, and also the nature of the culprit himself, who is my brother (not in the physical sense, but as a fellow creature similarly endowed with reason

and a share of the divine); therefore none of those things can injure me, for nobody can implicate me in what is degrading. Neither can I be angry with my brother or fall foul of him; for he and I were born to work together, like a man's two hands, feet or eyelids, or the upper and lower rows of his teeth. To obstruct each other is against Nature's law – and what is irritation or aversion but a form of obstruction."

2. "Too many rules get in the way of leadership. They just put you in a box . . . . People set rules to keep from making decisions." - Coach K

Made famous by the movie "Moneyball" and expounded upon by sportswriters everywhere, "Adapt or die" could be a tagline of the 21st century, of any century for that matter. Human beings adapt, it's how we have survived as long as we have. The caveman that adopted the stick lived to eat another day, the teams that adopted the spread offense made it to the finals.

There was a time in basketball when back to the basket centers like Shaquille O'Neal and Tim Duncan dominated the game. Today, a center that cannot shoot is a defensive liability, and only plays one way is unemployed. While extensive rule changes aided in this evolution of the game, so too did the ability of players to shoot the three ball. The point? The game has changed.

Coach K began his career at Duke in 1980 after five years with Army basketball. The difference between basketball in 1980 and 2019 is about the same as an Apple computer then and an iMac now.

In the early years, a player had to complete all four years of college before leaving for the NBA. This meant players like Michael Jordan, and Charles Barkley spent long careers in the NCAA before moving to the pros. This also meant that the game was vastly different in competition.

Coach K understands this better than anyone. He began his coaching career during the time of four-year starters. Players like Grant Hill, Christian Laettner, Shane Battier, Jay Williams, Mike Dunleavy Jr., Carlos Boozer epitomized this model. Duke was a team of men against boys.

He built his teams around Seniors, senior leadership, and the time to develop a player from a Freshman to a leader. There is a big difference between an 18-year-old phenom and a 22-year-old senior. During the back to the basket era of the ball, this was painfully obvious. To compete in basketball during this time, when hand checking was legal and fouls amongst the trees of bigs was kosher as locks and bagels, teams had to be tough, experienced, and disciplined. It was also a time when players such as Kevin Garnett, Kobe Bryant, Lebron James would go straight to the NBA; however, in 2006 all that changed as the NBA ruled that a player must play at least one year in basketball.

Why is this a big deal? The game changed instantly. Suddenly, the best players in the world were mandated to play at least one year in the NCAA, but no more. And with that decision, the one-and-done era began. This led to players like Kevin Durant playing one year in college and dominating the competition and whole teams like John Calipari's 2012 National Championship team led by freshman center Anthony Davis.

Coach K no longer was afforded the time to develop his players over four years, but rather, had to adapt to the new rules of the NCAA. For Coach K, this meant changing principles, coaching styles, and leadership skills. He had to learn to develop a team in one year, every year, as opposed to building it over several.

The result? Since 2006, Coach K has won two National Championships, five 30+ win seasons, and three conference championships. In other words, he won. He found a way to win. He adapted. He thrived.

3. "It takes courage not only to make decisions but to live with those decisions afterward" - Coach K

All coaches learn to make tough decisions. It's part of the responsibility. The burden of benching a player for breaking the rules, sitting a star to teach a larger lesson, and owning a loss is a tough cross to bear.

A coach must embody the team he leads. Like Belichick, Coach K is Duke basketball. The court his team plays on is now named after him. He is a staple of the game and one who has changed the lives of hundreds of players, students, and coaches. Fans are attracted to success. Players are attracted to the opportunity. Writers are attracted to the story. All understand the gravitas of the character of Coach K.

As Coach K puts it, "When a leader takes responsibility for his own actions and mistakes, he not only sets a good example, he shows a healthy respect for people on his team."

The lesson here is simple, and one that would be championed by Dr. Peterson: own your choices. Every leader must carry the weight of the outcome of their decisions, good and bad. The sign of an excellent leader, the sign of a strong leader, is how they handle responsibility, adversity, and duty.

Perhaps it was Coach K's time at West Point, his time under Coach Knight, and his time leading the Cadets at Army, but he understands that value and character come first. So, to must, you know that building your moral compass, building your conscious, is as important as developing your mental toughness.

"When you are passionate, you always have your destination in sight, and you are not distracted by obstacles. Because you love what you are pursuing, things like rejection and setbacks will not hinder you in your pursuit. You believe that nothing can stop you!" - Coach K

Actionable Steps:

-Who are your current starting five? Who are the five people you spend the most time with? Who influences your life?
-Who is your all-star starting five? If you could spend a day with any five historical figures, celebrities, authors, whoever, who would they be?
-Who is a mentor in your life that has made a difference? What qualities did they possess which you could emulate?
-What leadership qualities do you admire in your boss? Which qualities could they be better in? If you were the captain, how would you steer the ship?

Day 24: Name

"Just for once let me look on you with my own eyes… You were right. You were right about me. Tell your sister you were right." - Darth Vader

Demons are easier to face when we name them. Like the dragon, Lucas created a literal monster when he made Vader. Part shadow, part samurai, part wizard, Vader represented everything we feared. And yet, once Vader was finally unmasked, he was a frail, old man who struck fear in no one. We build up our obstacles greater than they actually are. Name your demon, face your demon. The obstacle is the way. What is stopping you? Put a name to it. Write it down. Vanquish it.

Chapter 13:

"Remember that this moment is not your life, it's just a moment in your life. Focus on what is in front of you, right now. Ignore what it 'represents' or it 'means' or 'why' it happened to you." - Ryan Holiday

Ryan Holiday is a bit of a controversial figure. He is a writer and media strategist who apprenticed under Robert Greene, the author of "The 48 Laws of Power," and later became the director of marketing for American Apparel. It was his work with the apparel company that landed him in hot waters as he detailed his experience, and propaganda, in the book "Trust Me I'm Lying: Confessions of a Media Manipulator."

Yet, it was his follow up books, a sort of Saul to Paul transformation, 'The Obstacle is the Way," and "Ego is the Enemy" that landed him in this book as the two have been quoted by NFL coaches, athletes, celebrities and political leaders.

He writes, often, on the virtues of stoicism in everyday life. As Holiday describes, "The philosophy asserts that virtue (such as wisdom) is happiness and judgment be based on behavior, rather than words. That we don't control and cannot rely on external events, only ourselves and our responses."

In other words, turn obstacles into advantages and learn to control what you can and accept the things you cannot.

"The obstacle in the path becomes the path. Never forget, within every obstacle is an opportunity to improve our condition." - Ryan Holiday

There is a similar idea in the school of improvisation. In improv, performers are taught to "bring a brick," meaning don't try and create an entire scene in the beginning, just get started and offer an idea. Additionally, they are taught to confront problems and use them rather than avoid them.

At its core, Stoicism is about action. It is this active verbiage that makes it a practical philosophy as opposed to an armchair idea. History is littered with thinkers and practitioners of this school as well.

Frederick the Great, Montaigne and Cato were all influenced by the writings of Cato and Epictetus, as well as Thomas Jefferson, Adam Smith, and Theodore Roosevelt.

T.R. lived the life of temperance and self-control that is the stuff of dreams for stoic, coining lines like, "What such a man needs are not courage but nerve control, cool-headedness. This he can get only by practice," and, "We must all wear out or rust out, every one of us. My choice is to wear out."

Life is a question and what we choose to do is the answer. Life is not set up for ease of access, to grant us our every wish. Life itself is an obstacle. As Marcus Aurelius noted we accommodate, and we adapt.

"The impediment to action advances action. What stands in the way becomes the way." - Marcus Aurelius

Despite its bad rap in the media and its daunting look in historical textbooks, the practice offers insight into a virtue. Holiday, inspired by Aurelius, provides us with this idea, that every obstacle is an opportunity.

We have the choice to change our perspective, to welcome adversity and rise to the challenge.

"Failure shows us the way—by showing us what isn't the way." -Ryan Holiday

How many historical figures faced seemingly insurmountable odds? T.R. himself, a boy riddled with asthma and a soft upbringing, was determined to forge himself into iron. He, quite literally, wrote the story of his life by leaving his elitist family behind and taking up life as a cowboy, a war strategist, and finally a public servant. Would anyone believed that the boy with breathing problems would later become famous for being a President who boxed in the Oval Office?

Every great man faced opposition. Every great leader, writer, and artist is met with hard times. We can choose to blame our circumstances or trap ourselves in a negative mindset, or we can, like the Stoics, control our attitude and approach.

What blocks the path, becomes the path? We all like to think that successful people rode a meteoric rise to the top, that our favorite actor became an overnight success. What the media doesn't write about are the years an actor spent in obscurity working in regional theatre, local commercials, and bit parts. What we forget is authors write books, journals, and rejected screenplays long before one lands.

"Think progress, not perfection" - Ryan Holiday

Comparison is the thief of joy. For some reason, it is encoded in our DNA to compare ourselves to others, and social media has amplified that flaw tenfold. We want success now, without the work. We want knowledge now, without the research. We want to stand atop the mountain, without the climb.

What if we shifted the perspective? What if the journey became the means? Rather than racing from one goal to the next, we focus on the lessons to learn and the trials faced, then we develop meaning from the journey and the importance of the obstacle.

The dragon in mythology represents all of man's greatest fears. He is a snake, cat, bird, all our ancestral predators rolled into one. He is also the perennial villain in countless stories ranging from The Hobbit to numerous fairy tales and myths. Even in modern times, the legend continues to grow with the likes of Godzilla, an ancient being made powerful by modern mistakes.

The point is, this obstacle is timeless. Our ancestors created stories based around the summation of our greatest, primordial fears. Every hero needs a great villain, or else the story falls flat. Sherlock needs Moriarty. Batman needs the Joker. Superman needs Lex Luthor. The greater the hero, the greater the weight he must bear.

"It's okay to be discouraged. It's not okay to quit. To know you want to quit but to plant your feet and keep inching closer until you take the impenetrable fortress you've decided to lay siege to in your own life—that's persistence." - Ryan Holiday

As we grow, so to do our obstacles. As we rise, the challenges become harder. Video games understand this principle. Name one game that gets easier as you play it. As the protagonist moves from novice to master, the obstacles change from mundane to mountains.

Now, rather than looking at life as something we are gifted, or expecting results to come to us, what if we embraced the challenges in front of us, as the reason we set out upon the journey in the first place?

The pitfalls of writing a novel are a part of writing a book. The challenges of memorizing Hamlet and understanding his complexities are the trials of the actor. The most significant opponent awaits the most celebrated athlete.

"The universe changes; our life is what our thoughts make it." -Marcus Aurelius

Actionable Steps:

-What currently stands in your way? How does it define your journey?
-If you have yet to begin your journey, what pitfalls await you? What trials will you have to face?
-What is a challenge you can add to your life? In the gym? In your creative endeavors? If something is stopping you, why?

Day 26: Values

"Courage is the most important of all the virtues because, without courage, you can't practice any other virtue consistently." - Maya Angelou

What do you believe in? What are your eulogy virtues? We rush day to day doing jobs for other people, or, if we are lucky, building our own dreams. Still, during the race, we forget what is important in life. Are you the kind of person people refer to as, "The kind a man who would give you the shirt off his back?" What will others say of you when you die? What do you want them to say? Write down the five virtues you believe in and bring out the bigs guns. If hard work and ethical are your bag, write them down. If honesty and dependability fit your bill, then pay the check.

Chapter 14:

"I choose to live by choice, not by chance."
Miyamoto Musashi

Mental toughness is about seizing upon what you want. It is about determining your path and seeing your journey through to the end. It is the ability to make the difficult decisions and the discipline to work day in and day out towards what you want.

Miyamoto Musashi is as much myth as he is a man. He is the sword-saint of Japan, going undefeated in his lifetime as a duelist at 61-0. He was a samurai, a philosopher, a strategist in the line of Sun Tzu, yet it is his writing that lived on long past his legend with "The Book of Five Rings," and "Dokkōdō" or "The Path of Aloneness."

While "The Book of Five Rings" serves as a warrior's treatise on combat and dueling, "The Path of Aloneness" lays its philosophical underpinnings. Both are masterful works on strategy, mindset, and war.

Either way, the man belongs among the ranks of Achilles and Odysseus, for he not only had the strength and training but the wit and wisdom to win again and again.

"Study strategy over the years and achieve the spirit of the warrior. Today is victory over yourself of yesterday; tomorrow is your victory over lesser men." - Musashi

The ronin's two-sword technique, a style he invented himself by studying drummers, was as straight forward has Musashi's advice. Like many warriors, he preferred simplicity to frills. "When you take up a sword, you must feel intent on cutting the enemy."

Yet, the warrior was complicated, studying Buddhism as well as the sword, along with arts such as calligraphy, art, and architecture, insisting a warrior should investigate other art forms, for, "If you know the Way broadly, you will see it in everything."

Musashi lived by the sword and held no pretensions over combat. Violence was precisely that, force, and the warrior focused as much on winning as on form. Death was his art, and he made his brush the most lethal.

What is there to learn from a 16th-century samurai whose most significant gift to mankind was a book on the subtleties of slaughter? What can we learn from a Ronin who perfected the code of Bushido?

Musashi's literal meaning on "the way of the sword" is meaningless today. Much like Sun Tzu's "The Art of War," the significance of how to hold a sword and defend with the two-handed technique belongs in the dojo and the classroom, not in the modern world. But, in between the parry and thrusts of Musashi's initial intent are the philosophical underpinnings of mental strength and meaning.

"Do not let the body be dragged along by mind nor be dragged along by the body." - Musashi

Musashi realized that the mind and body must be in sync, that we must have the purpose and the will to follow through with our goals. Below are quotes from the Master himself, each with a short explanation. Reflect upon each quote and how it relates to your life.

"There is nothing outside of yourself that can ever enable you to get better, stronger, richer, quicker, or smarter. Everything is within. Everything exists. Seek nothing outside of yourself." - Musashi

Often, we set out on a journey, on a path, for a teacher or an experience to change us. We seek a way to grow stronger, smarter, wealthier, more powerful. We seek something to fulfill us.

Marketing has learned this. Netflix has learned this. Masterclass and Udemy have learned this.

Don't get me wrong, there is nothing wrong with bettering yourself, hell, I am writing a book on improving yourself; however, what you need to learn is that the power to change lies within you.

If you meet the Buddha on the road, kill him. How many charlatans prey upon our weakness, our need for salvation? Buy this pill and your hair will be fuller, buy this class and you will be more productive, buy this, buy that, buy now.

You are enough. Yes, you must be willing to sacrifice, to grow, to change, but you must realize that change comes from within.

"The Way is in training." - Musashi

And yet, we must train. We must learn. We must keep the mind of a student to become the master. To realize you are enough is not to say you do not need to study. To find your inner strength is not to listen to those wiser than you. We can always improve and learn, as Josh Waitzkin noted, to draw "smaller and smaller circles."

"There is more to life than increasing its speed." - Musashi

With training comes understanding. We must learn that there is more to swordplay, more to life than improving one skill. Build upon your strengths but understand that man is not only a swordsman. He is a son, a father, a student, a teacher, an artist, and on and on. One man in his time plays many parts.

"Let it suffice to say that in Japan, a warrior carries two swords as a matter of duty, whether he knows how to use them or not. It is the Way of the warrior." - Musashi

We are all on a journey up the mountain. In any contest, as in life, there is never "one" combatant. Therefore, we must always be prepared to fight with a second tool, or, in other words, we must develop a second weapon. Musashi liked to refer to his writing as his "second sword." So, to must, you develop your mastery of one skill, your long sword, as well as find and develop your second sword. At some point an enemy will disarm you, and what then? Is the fight over? Have you no back up plan?

"Determine that today you will overcome yourself of the day before, tomorrow you will win over those of lesser skill, and later you will win over those of greater skill." - Musashi

The best measurement of a man is not the comparison to others but to himself. Are you better than you were yesterday? If so, you succeeded. If not, then saddle up and try and again tomorrow.

Instagram bombards us with people's handcrafted personal success stories. On social media, people are showing you their best selves. Do not compare your worst day to someone's highlight reel.

The only thing that matters is that today you got better. Today you moved toward your goal. Today you learned from failure, and tomorrow you will get better. Be better than you were yesterday, day by day, and you will master any enemy.

"To win any battle, you must fight as if you are already dead." -Musashi

Play every game like it's your last. Play likes there's no tomorrow. Our Little League coaches begged and pleaded with us with these mantras, yet, in our youth, we fail to realize that one day we will hang up the cleats, the racket, the sword.

For Musashi, he saw the only way to win was to prepare himself for death, to realize that the life he had chosen could only end one way.

While our day to day life may not be as epic as a Kurosawa duel, the sooner we realize that one day it will be all over, the sooner we will get moving. Medieval Christians had the practice of memento mori or reflecting on death. Each day set aside time to acknowledge your mortality and act as though one day the game will end.

As the Irish gravestone reads,

"Remember Man as you go by,
As you are now so once was I,
As I am now so shall you be,
Prepare yourself to follow me."

"Do nothing that is of no use" - Musashi

Once we define our purpose, everything we do should move us towards reaching our ends. While life takes wayward paths, we must direct our focus on what matters most to us.

"Think lightly of yourself and deeply of the world." - Musashi

Perhaps my favorite lesson from Musashi and a surprising one. A man who spent his life fighting to the death realized that to enjoy life honestly, you can't take yourself seriously. How many people do we know that can't take a joke? How many bosses have we had that cannot laugh? We all play the fool sometimes.

Actionable Steps:

-Learn swordsmanship. Just kidding but learn how to defend yourself. There is no greater self-confidence than learning you can hold your own. Find a class, find a course, study online, but study.

-Compete in something. Chess, video games, baseball, whatever, but play and compete.

Day 28: Gamble

"You know, horses are smarter than people. You never heard of a horse going broke betting on people." –Will Rogers

Musashi fought every battle as if it was his last. He lived his life as if every time he touched the sword he would die. Whether we want to admit it or not, life's a gamble. We do what we can to stack the deck in our favor but sometimes the odds are not in our favor. While the best throw of the dice is to throw them away, we do not have that choice in life. We must play the game. While I am not advocating picking up cards or betting the horses, I am recommending that you make friends with chance. When we place a bet, we are putting up value. So, rather than putting that money on something that could be potentially fruitless like Black 17, bet on yourself. Put your money on you. Call a friend and give them $50 and tell them if you do not complete a certain task by a certain time, then they get to keep. Watch how you move then.

Chapter 15:

"The game is afoot." -Sherlock Holmes

Children are born curious. As Neil deGrasse Tyson likes to say, all children are scientists. They absorb information like a sponge, learn new skills daily, and look at the world with fresh eyes. From school and sports to friends and social interactions, children are always being presented with new data, forcing them to be alert and tuned in.

Then, age comes in. The grey of life begins to wilt what was once colorful. Even Christmas, or whatever celebrations you may celebrate, begins to lose some of its shine. Suddenly, we've been there, done that, and already threw away the t-shirt. Suddenly, our sense of curiosity wanes and is replaced by mindless habits.

Since one thing is no longer enough, we begin multitasking-- despite all the data to the contrary. While we keep a sense of novelty, we lose the sense of wonderment. We search for more and more entertainment and less and less depth. Our attention spreads mile wide and an inch thick. The voices of podcasters, newscasters, bloggers, journalists, and a million other figures echoes in our head to the point that our own, unamplified voice cannot be heard.

"The world is full of obvious things which nobody by any chance ever observes." - Sherlock Holmes.

Enter that pipe smoking, violin playing, puzzle solving genius, Sherlock Holmes. Sir Arthur Conan Doyle's quintessential private detective has become the mold to which all others are held up: Batman, Poirot, Dr. House, Spok.

Holmes is remembered for his keen sense of observation, development of forensic science, deduction, and logical reasoning. First appearing in "A Study Scarlet" and initially plummeting to his death to stop his nemesis Moriarty in "The Final Problem" nothing captured the Victorian imagination quite like the world's first and only "consulting" detective. Yet, the character was too rich, to engaging to stay dead, and Doyle brought his character back from the grave, a tradition that continues today as countless plays, tv shows, and films are produced every year around the very idea of Sherlock Holmes.

Based on a combination of Doyle's mentor Dr. Joseph Bell and Edgar Allan Poe's detective Auguste Dupin, Holmes epitomizes strength of mind. Doyle took the qualities of his friend and combined them with the musings of Dupin, creating the most iconic intellectual of all time. Yet, it is not only Sherlock's intellect that attracts us but his ability to do what others are incapable of doing.

In his book "Thinking Fast and Slow" Daniel Kahneman puts forth the theory for the brain functioning under two systems, a real-time system in which we recognize speech and make "gut" decisions and a second system based around critical analysis of evidence.

Herein lies Holmes and Doyle's most significant contribution to mental strength: the mind attic. What we feed our brain, what we allow in, is what we will use to see the world. It is impossible to view the world without rose tinted glasses, we all have biases, judgments, and experiences. Whatever we allow in inevitably comes out, or, as Holmes puts it,

> "I consider that a man's brain originally is like a little empty attic, and you have to stock it with such furniture as you choose. A fool takes in all the lumber of every sort that he comes across, so that the knowledge which might be useful to him gets crowded out, or at best is jumbled up with a lot of other things so that he has difficulty in laying his hands upon it. Now the skillful workman is very careful indeed as to what he takes into his brain-attic. He will have nothing but the tools which may help him in doing his work, but of these, he has a large assortment and all in the most perfect order. It is a mistake to think that that little room has elastic walls and can distend to any extent. Depend upon it there comes a time when for every addition of knowledge, you forget something that you knew before. It is of the highest importance, therefore, not to have useless facts elbowing out the useful ones."

In this way we must treat our mind as a garden, tending to it regularly. We must choose what plants we allow in and what weeds we must pull. In essence, it is similar to how Charlie Munger, another mentally tough man whose books "Poor Charlie's Almanac" is a must-read, lays out mental models, or lattice. Munger was a proponent of mental models, much akin to Holmes' attic. He believed you should remember lessons and stories that will help you solve problems later in life and let the useless facts and junk make its way to the garbage heap.

Mixing metaphors, one must allow only the information they deem pertinent into their mind attic, and the stronger the models are to hang life lessons on the better. For Holmes, he put cases, analysis, and facts such as types of cigarette ash into his mental attic to allow him to solve the crime better. What do you let into your attic?

Sherlock not only has a mind attic, but also develops a literal memory palace. In order to retain what he learns, he treats memory like a location in order to access it. While this is the subject of a different book, it is still a useful tool to train your brain. If you're interested, check out the book "Moonwalking with Einstein."

Alongside developing a lean mental attic, Holmes offers us more useful tools to help build our mental strength.

First, the skill of observation.

"You see, but you do not observe. The distinction is clear." - Sherlock Holmes

One of Holmes favorite parlor tricks and a calling card of the character is his ability to observe a person in depth. At a single glance, he can deduce a person's location, age, occupation, and so on and so forth.

To do this, Holmes is using both forms of his brain, using intuitive sense connected with his more in-depth analysis. Most importantly, he is focusing on important details, deemed necessary by his brain attic. Like an elite athlete, Holmes focuses on what is essential and throws the rest out.

For Holmes, analysis and deduction are the most essential tools, although he does have many other useful habits. For an athlete like Tom Brady, it is a different set of skills. In fact, for Brady, he developed, along with his trainer Alex Guerrero, a system of working out individually for being a quarterback. The point being, elite performers, develop systematic approaches developed specifically for their needs, or in other words, they learn how to pay attention to what matters most.

Does a boxer need to deadlift 400 lbs.? Should a distance runner master the long jump? What about a chess master memorizing the entire *Star Wars* canonical universe? Mentally tough people learn to weed out the distractions, they learn what to say yes to and what to say no to. This is not to say they do have things outside their focus that bring them joy. After all, Lebron James is an avid wine connoisseur.

But top performers know how to focus. They also understand their attention, like willpower, is a limited resource. A human being can only accomplish so much in a day.

The second skill is analysis.

"It is a capital mistake to theorize before one has data. Insensibly one begins to twist facts to suit theories, instead of theories to suit facts." - Sherlock Holmes

The next thing that mentally tough people do is use both the process of their brain. They do not react to their active mind but allow the process to enter their slow analysis as well. They allow for observation but also an analysis of the facts.

We are constantly bombarded by information. Mentally tough people are not merely observers, they are analyzers and doers. They take in the data and then figure out how to use it. What does it mean? What is it connected to? What is it similar to? Have I seen this before? What was the outcome?

Furthermore, mentally tough people bridge the gap between the two. They learn to connect the two parts and turn their analysis into intuition, like Holmes. This is the world of mastery. How does a martial artist know where to defend next or a chess player think three moves ahead? How does a baseball player hit a 95-mph fastball but also sit back for the changeup? The key here is mastery.

Perhaps the most critical skill to develop is distance.

'I cannot live without brain-work. What else is there to live for?' - Sherlock Holmes

Holmes does not jump to conclusions. He allows for time. In the fast-paced world, we live in today where information can be shared in seconds, and the world let in secret instantly, we feel the constant need to produce. In fact, we so often put the cart in front of the horse that we expect product without process.

Yet, the world does not function this way. Things need time to develop. The average major league baseball players speed 3-5 years in the minors before moving up.

Just as ballplayers need time to grow, so to do thoughts need time to settle. How many people do you know that parrot whatever they heard on the radio, see on the news, or read from a blog? If they marinated on the information they've taken in, they would begin to see the flaws in their reasoning. Thus, the point presents itself.

Like meditation offers, we must learn to observe our thoughts. We must take a step back from the immediate action and analyze the moment. This will take time at first, but it will improve our decision making in the long run.

Sherlock has lived on past the Victorian era for a score of reasons, one of which is his mental toughness; however, at his core, he represents what is possible when a man dedicates himself fully to his passion. He not only mastered the art form, but he also invented it, "The World's First Consulting Detective."

Actionable Steps:

-To what event in your past did you react too quickly?
-What is an example of time presenting an answer?
-What information is key to your deeper understanding?

-Exercise: Build a mind palace.
   -Try out Holmes infamous memory palace, which he uses to remember data. Think of a place you know intimately well. What does it look like? What does it smell like? What does it feel like to be inside? Now, take a set of facts like a list of Presidents or your credit card number, and hang that information inside this memory.

Day 30: Finish Him

"We are what we repeatedly do. Excellence then is not an act, but a habit." - Aristotle

"Beware the barrenness of a busy life." - Socrates

You didn't think you would make it through a book about mental toughness without me mentioning Aristotle and Socrates, did you? The fathers of Western Philosophy always hit, and when they swing, they swing for the fences. The game is not over for you, but merely beginning. Keep learning, keep grinding, and know that you will be faced with greater trails. As Uncle Ben said, "With great power, comes great responsibility."

Conclusion

This is not some cheesy wrap up of this book. I am not going to write that after reaching this point your problems will be solved and your life without pain if anything by this point you understand I advocate the opposite. I want you to seek out the challenges and break through your limitations; however, there is an important thing we must all understand if we are to grow in our selected fields.

You are enough.

This is not a quote meant to rush you to social media and share with the gods of social conformity, nor is it the type of thing you paint on your wall. Some people love to take this sort of affirmative statements and make a mantra out of them, and if that's you, then go to.

What this is, however, is a reminder that you are the hero of your own life. You are the protagonist in your own movie and Superman is not going to show up and save you.

Some people hit the jackpot and are born lucky, some people attain greatest through connections or being at the right place at the right, and others have opportunity thrust upon them. For the rest of us, we must grind it out and develop beyond that level to which others have settled.

There are too many Instagrammers out there who post this sort of quotes next to pictures of their butts, odds are you may be one of those people looking to get a check up on the competition, and if so, then more power to you. But, for the rest of us, we must develop the confidence to deliver.

I do not mean that you should not work on yourself or that you do not need to grow and improve. Simply put, one of the greatest lessons we must all learn is that we are the solution to the problem.

Part of growing is learning who you are and what you are capable of achieving. Part of mental strength understands where you excel and where you are weak. Coach K knows how to build upon his team's strengths. Belichick understands how to mask his weaknesses and exploit his opponents. Bruce Lee uses his opponent's power against them. Every mentally strong person from Sherlock to Yoda understands themselves. As Socrates put it, "Know thyself," and as Shakespeare elaborated, "To thine own self be true."

We must ultimately learn to trust ourselves. We must learn to trust our intuition as well as our analysis. We must learn to develop the inner strength that carries us through the hard times, whether we borrow it from others or forge it on our own. Either way, we must become the mentor we wish to find.

There is no greater confidence than the ability to fully trust and be ourselves. That does not mean that we conquer all our demons, it merely means that we make peace with them and learn not to let them control our lives.

The point is that at the end of our journey the mana we bring back is the change within us. Once the hero brings the treasure back and shares it with the village, they assimilate back into everyday life, and yet, for every adventurer another journey awaits. New trials, new tests form once the hero is ready. Only this time, they are prepared with a new set of skills from battles previously won.

Are you ready?

Further Reading

"A Book of Five Rings" Miyamoto Musashi

"Grit" by Angela Duckworth

"Meditations" by Marcus Aurelius

"Extreme Ownership" by Jocko Willink

"Can't Hurt Me" by David Goggins

"The Art of War" by Sun Tzu

"The Artist's Way" by Julia Cameron

"12 Rules for Life" by Jordan B. Peterson

"The 48 Laws of Power" by Robert Greene

"The Obstacle is the Way" by Ryan Holiday

"How to Think Like Sherlock Holmes" by Maria Konnikova

"Man's Search for Meaning" by Viktor Fankl

"Mastermind: How to Think Like Sherlock Holmes" by Maria Konnikova

"Leading with the Heart" by Coach Mike Krzyzewski

"Start with Why" by Simon Sinek

"Getting Things Done" by David Allen

"The Seven Habits of Highly Effective People" by Stephen Covey

"Poor Charlie's Almanac" by Charles Munger

"The Prince" by Machiavelli

"Eleven Rings" by Phil Jackson

"The Art of Learning" by Josh Waitzkin

"10% Happier" by Dan Harris

"The One Thing" by Gary W. Keller and Jay Papasan

"Outliers" by Malcolm Gladwell

"Talent is Overrated" by Geoff Colvin

Afterword:

Thank you for reading this book. Thank you for making it this far and pushing through until the end. If you made it this far, consider this the "Bonus Track" that used to accompany the end of 90s albums.

Since you've come this far, I will not share the real "secret" with you. Are you ready? I asked you at the beginning of this book, but I knew you couldn't handle it without going on the journey. Now, here you are, at the last page, and either you read the whole damn thing, or, you skipped to the back to see the final chapter was interesting enough to spend your time on. If so, gotcha!

If not, then here it is, the secret: there is no secret.

No matter what people write, discover, or produce, there is no secret you are missing out on. We want to believe that the person who has what we have knows something we do not know or is privy to something we missed. We feel like we missed out on insider trading.

They even write books about there being a big "secret" that the world is missing out on, and people line up to buy it. Why? Because we want to believe in something bigger than ourselves. We want to pass the buck and say, "See, it wasn't my fault. I didn't know the secret."

Crackpot theorists and would be scholars spend hour after hour watching YouTube videos made by other crackpot theorists and reading blogs written by other would be scholars about how the Earth is flat, chemtrails are ruining our children, and the Illuminati have taken over the NBA. The point being, people want to believe there is a man behind the curtain, that someone is pulling the strings, and that we are all part of a big conspiracy.

Yet, all along we know the deeper truths. Like our instincts, there are some things ingrained so deeply in us that we can't explain them but know them to be true.

To be honest, the most mentally tough people I know are not always the CEOs and the Coaches, although success stories do inspire me. The toughest people I know are mothers and fathers, workers and day laborers, the men and women who grind every day to provide for a family. They are the men and women who make this country run, who get up every day, grab a cup of coffee, and go to work with a smile on their face. They make the people around them better and happier simply by being there. If you are looking for mental toughness, chat up the lady in your office who has kept the place glued together for 35 years while getting the kids to soccer practice, cooking dinner, helping a friend through rehab, and putting up with her husband not mowing the lawn, yet still finding time to tell you a joke and write you a Christmas card.

For humans, this is hard to compute. Everyday mundane things lose their luster quickly. They mesh into the background never to be seen again. This is why sports, stories, and history excite us. Suddenly, something matters.

The biggest lesson I ever learned from sports was that the game is just a metaphor. Everything we need to know about life, for the most part, can be learned between the lines; however, we so often forget that and winning takes precedence over lessons.

At some point it all comes to an end, and then what? What do we do with years of basketball practice, with years of perfecting a swing, a move, a routine? Do we drop the ball and never pick it back up? Is the game merely wasting time?

Similarly, the story holds the same argument. What is the point to "Star Wars", to "The Lord of the Rings", to "The Wizard of Oz"? Are they just escaping into another world where we trust everything will work itself out?

If you haven't figured out by now my answer is a resounding, "No," then I can't help you. Sports and stories give us insight into who we are without trying so hard. When our ancestors handed down myths of the gods, they were trying to pass on knowledge in a way we could retain it. When a great hunter or runner ascended beyond the tribe and became a legend our forefathers wanted to pass down his success to their children.

Now, this is not to say that a person can't sit back with a coffee and enjoy an episode of "Friends" and "Frasier" and forget about life for a while or crack open a few cold wins to watch the Sox play the Yankees. In fact, too often we tell ourselves, "We should be grinding right now," and lose sight of the love of the game. So many people are barking out us to "Work harder," "Work longer," "Be more productive," to the point that growth hacking and efficiency are the currency of the day.

What is a life if all we do is toil? The beauty of sports is while they are hard work, they are fun, and even though we are sweating in the grueling heat of the summer sun on a ballfield or pumping iron in a rusty gym, we are doing it for the thrill of competition and for the joy of play. Likewise, when we open a book, start a movie, or see a play we are experiencing mastery (hopefully) and brilliance of storytelling and the craft. On the flip side, an entire industry of writers, marketers, and advertisers spend dollar after dollar convincing you that you "deserve" to rest, that you "deserve" another beer, that you "deserve" to binge watch that series/ball game. We are a Nation that loves to be entertained. Then again, we are a Nation of storytellers.

My point? Balance. Don't think that you have to spend every waking hour cramming information down your throat, stress into your body, and money down the drain. Also, don't escape into the ether or streaming. Work hard, play hard.

Being mentally tough is about being able to crush it in the office, the gym, and at home. Being mentally tough is understanding that focus changes as you move from one phase to another. Being mentally tough is about living a life that people admire because you have the strength to make the tough decisions when they need to be made, whether that is in the boardroom or the bedroom.

Lastly, I love collecting knowledge. We have such a brief time here on this earth, that it is impossible to do everything.

Thus, man invented writing to pass on what he knew. After all, Otto Von Bismarck summed it up best with, "Only a fool learns from his own mistakes. The wise man learns from the mistakes of others."

Here are some thoughts, paraphrases, and general ideas that didn't quite make it into this book. They are more tools that may help you in your journey to building mental strength, they certainly helped me:

Expose yourself to as many new opportunities as possible
Everything you want in life is just outside your comfort zone; if it wasn't, you'd have it already.
Strive to have a growth mindset.
Live in a way that is congruent with your goals.
Take control of your own story.
Begin with the end in mind.
Find your passion, follow your bliss
Identify what's important so you can create a life that allows you to do important things.
Life's too short to do the things you suck at.
You've got to know where you're going before you make any decisions to go.
When you experience "crap" in your life, remember that farmers use manure as fertilizer.
Focus on progress, not perfection.
Start inside out with what resonates with you, your why, not outside in. Your why is your core.
Forge your own path, write your own how-to manual
All of the obstacles you face are the building blocks of your future success.

If you don't have a plan for yourself, you'll be a part of someone else's plan.

School does not dictate your life.

Your circumstances don't define you; rather they reveal you.

Find people who share your passion.

Build your reputation by helping others build theirs.

Guard your reputation at all costs, or, be do nothing that will ruin it

If you have time to whine and complain about something, then you have the time to do something about it.

Be remarkable, take risks. There is no room for ordinary.

Most people die when they are 27 but aren't buried until they're 77.

More people die on Monday at 9 am than any other day and time of the week.

Disregard irrelevant weaknesses.

Without passion, life is work. With passion, work is a hobby & life is the reward.

Empty and organize your thoughts regularly.

Make Lists. Do lists. Finish lists.

Sharpen the saw.

Focus on your eulogy virtues.

Memento mori.

Be better than people expect.

Be prepared.

Take notes.

You are better than "OK"

Say less than necessary.

It takes time.

Honor your natural rhythms.

Breathe.

Relax.

Drink water.
Eat for nutrition.
Move your body.
Be mindful of your environment.
Create one room full of beauty.
Read.
Write.
Listen.
Learn.
Rest.

This is the end, seriously. No more hidden chapters. No more tiny pushes in the right direction. It's up to you. Thank you for reading this book and thank you for making yourself better. Now, go out and live your life the way you see fit.